T0339473

Cambridge Elements ≡

Elements in the Philosophy of Law
edited by
George Pavlakos
University of Glasgow
Gerald J. Postema
University of North Carolina at Chapel Hill
Kenneth M. Ehrenberg
University of Surrey

HANS KELSEN'S NORMATIVISM

Carsten Heidemann
Schleswig-Holstein Bar Association

CAMBRIDGE
UNIVERSITY PRESS

CAMBRIDGE
UNIVERSITY PRESS

University Printing House, Cambridge CB2 8BS, United Kingdom

One Liberty Plaza, 20th Floor, New York, NY 10006, USA

477 Williamstown Road, Port Melbourne, VIC 3207, Australia

314–321, 3rd Floor, Plot 3, Splendor Forum, Jasola District Centre,
New Delhi – 110025, India

103 Penang Road, #05–06/07, Visioncrest Commercial, Singapore 238467

Cambridge University Press is part of the University of Cambridge.

It furthers the University's mission by disseminating knowledge in the pursuit of
education, learning, and research at the highest international levels of excellence.

www.cambridge.org
Information on this title: www.cambridge.org/9781108995221
DOI: 10.1017/9781108993661

© Carsten Heidemann 2022

First published 2022

A catalogue record for this publication is available from the British Library.

ISBN 978-1-108-99522-1 Paperback
ISSN 2631-5815 (online)
ISSN 2631-5807 (print)

Hans Kelsen's Normativism

Elements in the Philosophy of Law

DOI: 10.1017/9781108993661
First published online: January 2022

Carsten Heidemann
Schleswig-Holstein Bar Association

Author for correspondence: Carsten Heidemann, heidemann.carsten@gmail.com

Abstract: Hans Kelsen's *Pure Theory of Law* is the most prominent example of legal normativism. This Element traces its genesis. In philosophy, normativism started with Hume's distinction between Is-and Ought-propositions. Kant distinguished practical from theoretical judgments, while resting even the latter on normativity. Following him, Lotze and the Baden neo-Kantians instrumentalized normativism to secure a sphere of knowledge which is not subject to the natural sciences. Even in his first major text, Kelsen claims that law is solely a matter of Ought or normativity. In the second phase of his writings, he places himself in the neo-Kantian tradition, holding legal norms to be Ought-judgments of legal science. In the third phase, he advocates a barely coherent naive normative realism. In the fourth phase, he supplements the realist view with a strict will theory of norms, coupled with set pieces from linguistic philosophy; classical normativism is more or less dismantled.

Keywords: Kelsen, normativism, Kant, neo-Kantianism, validity

ISBNs: 9781108995221 (PB), 9781108993661 (OC)
ISSNs: 2631-5815 (online), 2631-5807 (print)

Contents

1 Introduction   1

2 The Genesis of Normativism in Philosophy   2

3 Hans Kelsen's Normativism   23

4 Summary   72

References   75

1 Introduction*

Normativism is an important strand in philosophy. It can roughly be defined as having three basic features. First, there is a fundamental mode of Ought, or normativity, which cannot be reduced to the mode of Is, or factuality. Second, normativity is in some way objective. Third, normativity is constitutive of a certain domain, be it ontology, epistemology, language, morality, or law.

In accordance with the third feature, philosophical normativism is not restricted to securing the objectivity and autonomy of the 'practical' sphere; it also plays an important role in metaphysics. As will be shown (Section 2.2.2), Kant's rejection of transcendental realism without succumbing to skepticism was only possible by his adopting a variety of normativism for his theoretical philosophy. In present-day philosophy, normativism dominates not only parts of the theory of meaning in a narrow sense; it is also central to Hilary Putnam's internal realism, Jürgen Habermas's discourse theory, and Robert Brandom's inferentialism – to name some prominent examples.

Normativism in legal theory is mainly associated with the writings of Hans Kelsen (1881–1973). While there is scarcely any legal theorist who would subscribe to its tenets without restrictions, the Pure Theory of Law gained worldwide recognition and had an impact on authors like H. L. A. Hart, Joseph Raz, and Robert Alexy. The normativistic tendencies of current legal theory are generally due to Kelsen's immediate or mediated influence. But Kelsen's texts represent not only what might be called the 'historical core' of legal normativism; having undergone several changes of paradigm during the long span of time in which they were published, they also give an overview of a broad range of divergent aspects of normativism. All of this justifies a closer look at his theory.

The term 'normativism' seems to owe at least part of its currency to Kelsen's theory. It is comparatively young. The German equivalent, *Normativismus,* had been in use since the nineteenth century; it gained prominence after it was introduced into legal theory, by the right-wing legal philosopher Carl Schmitt, as a pejorative 'battle term,' when polemicizing against Kelsen's theory of law in the 1930s.[1] Schmitt saw normativism in law as the view that law is exclusively a system of (normative) rules which are objective, impersonal, and independent of factuality (Schmitt 1977: 370–1). This definition captures fairly well the three aspects mentioned above and what Kelsen probably had in mind as the lowest common denominator of his different conceptions of normativism.

* I am grateful to two anonymous reviewers for helpful remarks. Special thanks go to Monika Zalewska for our enriching discussion of Kelsenian and philosophical topics.
[1] On the Kelsen–Schmitt controversy, see Paulson 2017.

In the second section of this Element, the development of the Is–Ought dualism and normativism in philosophy is traced, by sketching some historical 'landmarks' which informed Kelsen's theory. This is necessary because the meaning and role of 'Ought' can hardly be understood without drafting the history of this concept – unless one is content with the meagre and apodictic explanation of the dualism Kelsen gave in the second edition of *Pure Theory of Law*:

> The difference between is and ought cannot be explained further. We are immediately aware of the difference. Nobody can deny that the statement 'something is' – that is, the statement by which an existent fact is described – is fundamentally different from the statement: 'something ought to be' – which is the statement by which a norm is described. (Kelsen 2005: 5–6 [Kelsen 1960: 5])

In the third section, the genesis of Kelsen's version of normativism is sketched. His first major text, *Hauptprobleme der Staatsrechtslehre* (1911), is treated comparatively extensively. It contains the germs of Kelsen's later Pure Theory of Law while connecting it to the jurisprudential tradition of the nineteenth century; besides, though little known, it is a true specimen of normativism in its own right.

Both the second and third sections concentrate on neo-Kantianism for three reasons. First, neo-Kantianism is the predecessor of modern analytical philosophy; the Baden school developed normativism as a metaphysical theory in a highly sophisticated manner so that it still informs present-day discourse.[2] Second, Kelsen's theory emerged at a time when neo-Kantianism impregnated German academic culture. It incorporated neo-Kantian theorems 'subcutaneously' from the beginning and is not intelligible without this theoretical surrounding. Third, Kelsen's explicitly neo-Kantian writings from the 1920s, especially *Das Problem der Souveränität*, *Der soziologische und der juristische Staatsbegriff* and *Rechtswissenschaft und Recht*, though philosophically his best, are not well known; they are written in a difficult style and have not been translated into English.

Finally, the fourth section gives a short summary of the findings of sections two and three.

2 The Genesis of Normativism in Philosophy

2.1 Hume's Law

Hume's Law is the starting point of the modern discussion of the dualism of Is and Ought.[3] Although the notion that there is some form of normativity is

---

[2] On this topic, see the instructive paper Beiser 2009: 9–37.

[3] However, in secondary literature both whether Hume's text is the origin of the philosophical tradition of a dualism between Is and Ought and what Hume really meant is contested; see the seminal paper McIntyre 1959: 451–68.

millennia-old, so that saying something is valuable, obligatory, or ought to be the case is not just a statement of fact, it is only since David Hume (1711–76) that it has been an explicit topos of philosophy that norms cannot be deduced from nature, or Is-propositions.

Hume, together with Kant and Wittgenstein, is one of the great innovators of modern philosophy (if it is deemed to be an analytical enterprise) insofar as he tries to completely reform metaphysics, doing away with any elements which have a supernatural flavor. Hume's classic formulation of the dualism of Is and Ought runs as follows:

> In every system of morality, which I have hitherto met with, I have always remarked, that the author proceeds for some time in the ordinary way of reasoning, and establishes the being of a God, or makes observations concerning human affairs; when of a sudden I am surprised to find, that instead of the usual copulations of propositions, is, and is not, I meet with no proposition that is not connected with an ought, or an ought not. This change is imperceptible; but is, however, of the last consequence. For as this ought, or ought not, expresses some new relation or affirmation, 'tis necessary that it should be observed and explained; and at the same time that a reason should be given, for what seems altogether inconceivable, how this new relation can be a deduction from others, which are entirely different from it. But as authors do not commonly use this precaution, I shall presume to recommend it to the readers; and am persuaded, that this small attention would subvert all the vulgar systems of morality, and let us see, that the distinction of vice and virtue is not founded merely on the relations of objects, nor is perceived by reason. (Hume 2007a: 302)

This is 'Hume's Law', usually summarized as saying that it is impossible to deduce Ought-propositions from Is-propositions. But actually the text is richer than that. It comprises different claims. First, Is and Ought are "copulations of propositions" (*a is b* vs. *a ought to be b)*. Second, Ought-propositions concern morality, God, or human affairs. Third, it seems to be inconceivable (though perhaps a reason might be given) that Ought-propositions could be deduced from Is-propositions, because the Ought-denotes some "new relation or affirmation." Fourth, Ought-propositions cannot be validated by "relations of objects" or by reason.

Hume does not argue for these claims; he seems to take them as self-evident. The short passage quoted above more or less exhausts what he has to say concerning the subject; the dualism does not play a vital role in his theory, nor is Hume consequent in observing it. In his philosophical system, the Is–Ought dualism results in skepticism concerning the objectivity of moral propositions, because Hume only accepts two categories of objective knowledge, namely, "relations of ideas" (expressed by analytical/mathematical sentences) and "matters of fact" (expressed by empirical sentences) (Hume 2007b: 18). Accordingly, his description of the Is–Ought distinction differs in two (possibly contradictory) points from the provisional definition of normativism given above. Ought-propositions, for him, are not objective; and he does not altogether exclude the possibility that there might be a derivation of Ought from Is, after all.

2.2 Normativism in Kant's Critique of Reason

Immanuel Kant (1724–1804) shares the critical concern of revising metaphysics with the aim of purifying it from any supernatural elements. His approach, however, is different from Hume's. To put it simply, Hume's perspective is that of an observer of 'human nature'; he analyzes the elements of cognition from the outside, so that cognition seems, to him, to be a matter of associations of perceptions. Kant's philosophy, on the other hand, starts – as it were – inside cognition and explores the necessary conditions for the possibility of objective judgments – it is the perspective of a participant. And while Hume radicalizes the theories of his empiricist predecessors by jettisoning rationalist elements, Kant seeks a synthesis between rationalism and empiricism by assigning both empirical and rational elements their proper place in cognition.

Kant advocates the thesis that Ought-judgments cannot be reduced to or deduced from Is-judgments without referring to Hume in this context (of course, he explicitly mentions him when confessing that it was Hume who aroused him from his "dogmatic slumber" (Kant 2004: 10 [A 13]). This is understandable considering the background that normativity plays a different and more important role in Kant's philosophy than in Hume's. His transcendental idealism tries to steer a middle path between empiricism and rationalism in order to avoid Humean skepticism, and normativity plays an important part in this project. Kant points to normativity to strictly separate practical questions from empirical or theoretical ones. But Kant is also the first major philosopher to turn the tables and hold not only that Ought-propositions cannot be reduced to Is-propositions; rather, any kind of theoretical or Is-cognition presupposes normativity. For him, practical reason has, in several ways, priority over theoretical reason.

2.2.1 The Distinction between Is and Ought

Kant maintains explicitly that there is no way of deriving what ought to be (done) from natural facts. Conversely, the Ought is meaningless when dealing with proceedings in nature. To describe this state of affairs, he uses terminology very similar to that which Kelsen employed some 150 years later:

> The ought expresses a species of necessity and a connection with grounds which does not occur anywhere else in the whole of nature. In nature the understanding [*Verstand*] can cognise only what exists, or has been, or will be. It is impossible that something in it ought to be other than what, in all these time-relations, it in fact is; indeed, the ought, if one has merely the course of nature before one's eyes, has no significance whatever. We cannot ask at all what ought to happen in nature, any more than we can ask what properties a circle ought to have; but we must rather ask what happens in nature, or what properties the circle has. (Kant 1998: 540 [A 547])

This passage contains some further qualifications of the Ought which are not important in this context, but which are noteworthy: The Ought goes along with a kind of necessity, and it expresses a "connection with grounds," not with causes.

In another passage in the *Critique of Pure Reason*, Kant maintains:

> Whereas, so far as nature is concerned, experience supplies the rules and is the source of truth, in respect of the moral laws it is, alas, the mother of illusion! Nothing is more reprehensible than to derive the laws prescribing what ought to be done from what is done, or to impose upon them the limits by which the latter is circumscribed. (Kant 1998: 398 [A 318–19/B 375])

Like Hume, in both passages Kant does not further argue for this point, but seems to take it to be self-evident. Finally, in the *Critique of Judgment,* regarding the sphere of practical reason, Kant holds:

> Now since . . . the objective necessity of the action, as duty, is opposed to that which it, as an occurrence, would have if its ground lay in nature and not in freedom (i.e., in the causality of reason), and the action which is morally absolutely necessary can be regarded physically as entirely contingent (i.e., what necessarily should happen often does not), it is clear that it depends only on the subjective constitution of our practical faculty that the moral laws must be represented as commands (and the actions which are in accord with them as duties), and that reason expresses this necessity not through a be (happening) but through a should-be, which would not be the case if reason without sensibility (as the subjective condition of its application to objects of nature) were considered, as far as its causality is concerned, as a cause in an intelligible world, corresponding completely with the moral law, where there would be no distinction between what should be done and what is done, between a practical law concerning that which is possible through us and the theoretical law concerning that which is actual through us. (Kant 2002: 273 [A 338–9/B 342-3])

Compared to the previously cited passages, which are pleasantly clear, this one seems obscure and needs some explanation. What Kant seems to mean, as far as our topic is concerned, is that the Ought (or the moral law) expresses what is morally necessary, in contradistinction to the natural law which expresses what is physically necessary. That which is morally necessary may be the case or may not be the case; only in an "intelligible world," that is, an ideal world in which all norms are complied with (a deontically perfect world), is everything that ought to be the case really the case – norms and natural laws would be one. And Kant insinuates some other important points that he elaborates elsewhere and which have an impact on Kelsen's conception: The Ought emanates from reason; that is why it is on the one hand subjective (having its origin in a faculty of mind) and on the other hand objective in the sense of being 'reasonable.' So (pure) reason has two different functions – a theoretical (speculative) one, directed at "the cognition of the object up to the highest a priori principles," and a practical one, directed at "the determination of the will with respect to the final and complete end" (Kant 2015: 97 [A 216]). Further, the Ought is expressive of "freedom," defined as independence from causal laws. Accordingly, the Ought-laws are contrasted with natural laws; and by complying with norms, a "causality by freedom" originates.

2.2.2 The Primacy of Ought over Is

Although Is and Ought have to be kept apart, there are, for Kant, at least two relations between them where the Ought is logically prior to the Is. First, there is a "primacy" of practical reason over theoretical reason. Second, understanding's activity of judging presupposes a minimum of autonomy and, thus, of normativity.

2.2.2.1 The Primacy of Practical Reason

Kant explains the possibility of a primacy of the practical function of pure reason over its theoretical function as follows:

> If practical reason may not assume and think as given anything further than what speculative reason of itself could offer it from its insight, the latter has primacy. Supposing, however, that practical reason has of itself original a priori principles with which certain theoretical positions are inseparably connected, while these are withdrawn from any possible insight of speculative reason (although they must not contradict it): then the question is, which interest is supreme (not, which must give way, for one does not necessarily conflict with the other)?[4] (Kant 2015: 97 [A 216])

And the "practical interest" of reason overrides, because it involves original principles a priori which are practically necessary and insofar proven, but

---

[4] "Interest," in this context, is defined by Kant as "a principle that contains the condition under which alone [the] exercise [of a faculty of mind] is promoted" (Kant 2015: 97 [A 216]).

theoretically undecidable; they consist of the moral law, which is a "fact of reason," and its presuppositions (the "practical postulates," freedom, immediately, and immortality of the soul and God in a mediated way) – or so I read Kant.[5] This is a metaphysically demanding relation between Is and Ought which need not be discussed any further in the present context, because it presupposes the complex conceptual edifice of Kant's explanation of reason and has no impact on Kelsen's theory.

2.2.2.2 The Spontaneity of Understanding

There is, however, a less obvious role for normativity in Kant's *Critique of Pure Reason* which also indicates a primacy of Ought over Is. Kant's explanation of 'understanding' (*Verstand*) is probably the first major attempt at a normativistic theory of cognition. In fact, it is easy to see why some conception of normativity, or rules, should be fundamental to Kant's theoretical philosophy as soon as one considers the argument that triggered his transcendental idealism. To be sure, the *Critique of Pure Reason* sets out to vindicate the possibility of synthetic judgments a priori, i. e. of judgments that extend our knowledge but which are not dependent on experience; yet Kant's transcendental idealism is foremost an answer to the aporias of philosophical realism, that is, of a position according to which cognition deals with objects which are independent of it:

> Truth, it is said, consists in the agreement of cognition with its object. In consequence of this mere nominal definition, my cognition, to count as true, is supposed to agree with its object. Now I can compare the object with my cognition, however, only by cognizing it. Hence my cognition is supposed to confirm itself, which is far short of being sufficient for truth. For since the object is outside me, the cognition in me, all I can ever pass judgement on is whether my cognition of the object agrees with my cognition of the object. The ancients called such a circle in explanation a *diallelon*. And actually the logicians were always reproached with this mistake by the sceptics, who observed that with this explanation of truth it is just as when someone makes a statement before a court and in doing so appeals to a witness with whom no one is acquainted, but who wants to establish his credibility by maintaining that the one who called him as witness is an honest man. (Kant 1992: 557–8)

Kant tackles this problem not by succumbing to skepticism, but by dissolving metaphysics into epistemology: "The proud name of an ontology . . . must give way to the modest one of a mere analytic of the pure understanding" (Kant 1998: 57–8 [A 247/B 303–4]). He dismisses the idea that the truth and objectivity of judgments are guaranteed by their referring to a transcendent reality and

---

[5] This topic is discussed elaborately in Willaschek 2009.

holds that they are instead the result of an interaction between receptive or passive sensibility and the spontaneous activity of understanding (*Verstand*). Other candidates not being available, this spontaneity is made up by understanding's activity – that is, thinking or judging – being guided by rules, and by the judging subject's competence to distinguish correct from incorrect applications of these rules.

There are quite a number of passages where this indispensable normativist level of Kant's theory emerges – for example, when he explains concepts as rules for uniting representations, or when he defines understanding generally as the "faculty of rules" (*Vermögen der Regeln*) (Kant 1998: 242 [A 126]). In fact, Kant's theoretical philosophy might presuppose a solution of the third antinomy (Willaschek 2010: 165–84). That is, in short, the cognitive constitution of the world of objects might presuppose some form of freedom of will, or normativity.[6]

Against this background, it is not astonishing that, for Kant, logic is concerned with normative rules: "In logic, however, the question is not about contingent but about necessary rules; not how we do think, but how we ought to think" (Kant 1992: 529). In a similar vein, borrowing from the language of jurists, he distinguishes between questions of what is lawful (*quid juris*) and questions of fact (*quid facti*) (Kant 1998: 219–20 [A 84/B 116]), that is, between empirical questions and questions of justification, or genesis and validity.

What is noteworthy about this kind of 'theoretical normativity' is that, unlike moral normativity, it does its work implicitly. Kant describes it in a way which is close to Wittgenstein's explanation of the phenomenon of rule following. In the *Jäsche-Logik*, Kant holds:

> The exercise of our powers also takes place according to rules that we follow, *unconscious* of them at first, until we gradually arrive at cognition of them through experiments and lengthy use of our powers, indeed, until we finally become so familiar with them that it costs us much effort to think them *in abstracto*. Thus universal grammar is the form of a language in general, for example. One speaks without being acquainted with grammar, however; and

---

[6] Cf., in the same direction, Walker 2017: 205: "So, after all, does not theoretical reasoning provide as sound a basis for presupposing freedom as practical reasoning does? [Kant] seems to be suggesting this in the *Groundwork*, when he says '*one cannot possibly think of a reason that would consciously receive direction from any other quarter with respect to its judgments, since the subject would then attribute the determination of his judgment not to his reason but to an impulse. Reason must regard itself as the author of its principles independently of alien influences, consequently, as practical reason or as the will of a rational being, it must be regarded of itself as free.*' This makes it seem as though the same case can be made for autonomy in judging as in acting, though he is here appealing only to how one must think of oneself. One might wonder why he never develops the idea."

he who speaks without being acquainted with it does actually have a grammar and speaks according to rules, but ones of which he is not himself conscious. Like all our powers, *the understanding* [*Verstand*] in particular is bound in its actions to rules, which we can investigate. (Kant 1992: 527 [A 2])

The most remarkable feature of these rules is that, although they can in principle be made explicit or "thought of *in abstracto*," in their basic form they are not 'objects' to be applied in certain situations; rather, they are just *implicit* in certain acts: This is the only interpretation that takes care of Kant's thesis that you can have a grammar without knowing it. It anticipates Wittgenstein's famous dictum: "When I follow the rule, I do not choose. I follow the rule blindly" (Wittgenstein 2009: 92 [219]).

This interpretation is underpinned by Kant's text on schematism, where he discusses the problem of how an intuition might be subsumed under a concept. That poses a problem because intuitions and concepts are heterogeneous (*ungleichartig*), stemming from different cognitive faculties. Concepts – or the judgments which employ them – are the result of exerting the spontaneous faculty of understanding, while intuitions stem from the passive faculty of sensibility. Kant's solution is that an intuition and a concept can be related to each other by applying a scheme, which is a

> rule for the determination of our intuition, in accordance with some specific universal concept. The concept "dog" signifies a rule according to which my imagination can delineate the figure of a four-footed animal in a general manner, without limitation to any single determinate figure such as experience, or any possible image that I can represent *in concreto*, actually represents. This schematism of our understanding, in its application to appearances and their mere form, is an art concealed in the depths of the human soul, whose real modes of activity nature is hardly ever likely to allow us to discover, and to have open to our gaze. (Kant 1998: 273–4 [A 141/B 180–1])

Concepts, therefore, signify rules, and schematism guides their application in a way which is not a possible subject of reflection. Accordingly, in the introduction to the chapter on schematism Kant says that if logic claims to show, universally,

> how we are to subsume under these rules, that is, to distinguish whether something does or does not come under them, that could only be by means of another rule. This, in turn, for the very reason that it is a rule, again demands guidance from judgment. And thus it appears that, though understanding is capable of being instructed, and of being equipped with rules, judgment is a peculiar talent which can be practised only, and cannot be taught. (Kant 1998: 268 [A 133/B 172])

Some lines later on Kant maintains that a physician, lawyer, or politician

> may have at command many excellent pathological, legal, or political rules,
> even to the degree that he may become a profound teacher of them, and yet,
> none the less, may stumble in their application. For, although admirable in
> understanding, he may be wanting in natural power of judgment. . . . Or the
> error may be due to his not having, through examples and actual practice,
> adequate training for this particular act of judgment. (Kant 1998: 268–9 [A
> 134/B 173])

This is, again, a striking anticipation of Wittgenstein's rule-following con-
siderations – even as far as the terminology is concerned. Kant recognizes the
problem of applying a rule, if taken to be an object, to its "material"; he
discusses the problem of an infinite regress of rules/interpretations, and he
deems a competent application of a rule to be a question of "training." These
arguments are at the core of Kant's theoretical philosophy, because any cognition of an object presupposes the correct application of the categories; and
categories, being pure concepts of understanding, are, like all concepts, rules
which are applied in the procedure of schematizing. Since, for Kant, classical
ontology dissolves into an analytic of understanding, we might say that, for
a Kantian-minded philosophy, implicit normativity is one of the most basic
elements of any metaphysics.

2.2.3 Relations between Is and Ought

Although Is and Ought are fundamentally different functions of reason, there
are, for Kant, several relations between them. First, as was shown in
Section 2.2.2, the "primacy" of practical reason postulates the existence of
freedom, the immortality of the soul, and God which, for theoretical reason,
were just a possibility. Second, the cognition of any natural object (and thus the
possibility of nature itself) presupposes a set of implicit rules guiding cognition,
the 'theoretical Ought.' Third, there is a structural analogy between laws of
nature and practical laws. Fourth, the categorical imperative is a rule guiding the
choice of maxims, thus influencing the empirical will. Fifth, any act that is
exerted by following such a maxim, which is in accordance with the categorical
imperative, starts a new chain of "causality from freedom." Sixth, any Ought
aims at producing a certain state of affairs, and this state of affairs must be
possible:

> Now although there is an incalculable gulf fixed between the domain of the
> concept of nature, as the sensible, and the domain of the concept of freedom,
> as the supersensible, so that from the former to the latter (thus by means of the
> theoretical use of reason) no transition is possible, just as if there were so

many different worlds, the first of which can have no influence on the second: yet the latter should have an influence on the former, namely the concept of freedom should make the end that is imposed by its laws real in the sensible world; and nature must consequently also be able to be conceived in such a way that the lawfulness of its form is at least in agreement with the possibility of the ends that are to be realized in it in accordance with the laws of freedom. (Kant 2002: 63 [A/B XIX])

2.3 Normativity and Validity: Lotze and the Neo-Kantians

Kant's thesis of a primacy of practical reason was taken up and radicalized in the highly idiosyncratic theory of Johann Gottlieb Fichte (1762–1814), who influenced especially the neo-Kantians of the Baden school, but made no important contribution to elucidating the concepts of normativity and validity. However, the theory of validity of Hermann Lotze (1817–81) had an enormous impact on neo-Kantian and later analytical philosophy, influencing among others Wilhelm Windelband, Heinrich Rickert, Edmund Husserl, and Gottlob Frege – and informing Kelsen's conception of normative validity. Lotze's influence lingers on in current normativistic philosophy; accordingly, he has aptly been called "the grandfather of the concept of normativity, which has become such a mantra in contemporary philosophy" (Beiser 2013: 127).

2.3.1 Hermann Lotze

Both a physician and a philosopher, Lotze published his main works in the middle of the nineteenth century, at a time when philosophical idealism had lost ground in Germany (as had philosophy in general), natural sciences were more and more successful, and psychology was getting established as a science. Lotze's ambition was to reconcile natural sciences and idealism in a system which he called "teleological idealism." And like Kant and Fichte, although in a different way, Lotze assumes a primacy of practical over theoretical philosophy.[7] In an early text, he defines his position as follows:

> [The appearances] come and emerge, held and connected not by some external object, but by their interrelation, which a higher power without needing material forces for its acts has prescribed. Our study has dissolved into this *teleological idealism*. . . . [T]he beginning of metaphysics is not in itself, but in ethics. (Lotze 1841: 329, my translation)

The first part of the quotation sounds almost Kantian; the difference is that objectivity is not derived from the correct application of the

---

[7] On this topic, see Thieme 1887.

concepts of understanding, but from a higher power which Lotze labels the value of "the good" (*das Gute*) (Lotze 1841: 324–6). Cognition aims at this value; that is why Lotze's theory may be termed a 'teleological' variant of idealism.

An important means in Lotze's endeavor to reconcile natural sciences and idealism is the concept of "validity," in contradistinction to "existence." Existence is the way natural objects are given; validity is the normative way values, truths, or true judgments are given. It is a basic, undefinable metaphysical concept: "[W]e must not ask what in its turn is meant by Validity, with any idea that the meaning which the word conveys clearly to us can be deduced from some different conception" (Lotze 1884: 440).

Validity is not subjected to space and time. Its normative character is not stressed by Lotze; however, it is a consequence of his combination of idealism with the view that "truths" or true judgments must not be hypostatized. And he maintains, when dealing with Descartes, that there is a "matter or content of our cogitation, which supplies not only the original datum from which we start, but the sole source from which that which we ought to think or that which we cannot but think can be derived" (Lotze 1884: 454). This normative "matter of our cogitation" is a "valid truth." From such metaphysical priority of normativity, Lotze shapes one of the first powerful normativistic post-Kantian arguments against psychologism (i.e. the view that logic and epistemology might be reduced to psychology):

> What particular tone of mind is required for successful thinking, how the attention is to be kept up, distraction avoided, torpidity stimulated, precipitation checked, all these are questions which no more belong to the field of logic than do enquiries about the origin of our sense-impressions and the conditions under which consciousness in general and conscious activity is possible. We may presuppose the existence of all these things, of perceptions, ideas, and their connexions according to the laws of a psychical mechanism, but logic only begins with the conviction that the matter cannot end here; the conviction that between the combination of ideas, however they may have originated, there is a difference between truth and untruth, and that there are forms to which these combinations *ought* to answer and laws which they *ought* to obey. It is true that we may attempt by a psychological investigation to explain the origin of this authoritative consciousness itself; but the only standard by which the correctness of our results could be measured would be one set up by the very consciousness to be investigated. The first thing, then, that has to be ascertained is, *what* the contents of this authoritative conviction are; the history of its growth can only have the second place, and even then must conform to requirements of its own imposing. (Lotze 1884: 7–8)

The importance of this passage cannot be overvalued; it signifies a different thrust of the argument from the dualism of Is and Ought. While Hume and, in his practical philosophy, Kant, made use of the argument to delimit the practical from the theoretical sphere, Lotze uses it to show that there cannot be a purely naturalist or psychologist explanation of cognition, because any combination of ideas in a judgment presupposes that this combination is either correct or incorrect, valid or invalid, so that it is subjected to normative standards. Kant advocated a similar thesis (as shown in Section 2.2.2), but it does not explicitly play an important role in his philosophy. This is not so in Lotze's conception: When he developed his theory in the middle of the nineteenth century, philosophy faced its own fragmentation and the onslaught of the successful natural sciences. Normativism seemed to be the only way to preserve the autonomy of the humanities and philosophy itself; normative 'validity' designated a realm exempt from the grasp of the natural sciences because it was, in fact, a necessary presupposition for any scientific judgment.

If one takes into account this central historical role of normativism, it is not surprising that Lotze does not focus as much on the 'moral' or practical Ought. Although he planned to write a philosophy of morality, aesthetics, and religion as a third part of his *System der Philosophie,* it was never accomplished.

There is, however, one point where Lotze differs from the Kantian tradition as regards normativity. While Kant's notion of normativity is, foremost, one of Ought-rules which are not objects of any kind, Lotze explains the notion of validity by referring to Plato's doctrine of ideas. From the notion that the reality of a truth consists in its validity, according to Lotze,

> some light is thrown on a surprising statement which is handed down to us in the history of Philosophy. Plato, we are told, ascribed to the Ideas of which he had achieved the conception an existence apart from, things, and yet, as these same critics tell us, of like kind with the existence of things. ... The truth which Plato intended to teach is no other than that which we have just been expounding, that is to say, the validity of truths as such. ... But the Greek language then as afterwards was wanting in an expression for this conception of Validity as a form of Reality not including Being or Existence. (Lotze 1884: 440–1)

It was this assimilation of 'valid truths' to Platonic ideas that led some neo-Kantians, notably Heinrich Rickert, to ascribe validity – as will be shown in Section 2.3.2 – to "values," which are not norms directed at human subjectivity, but which have an objective reality independent from it. Although this does not seem to be quite in accordance with Lotze's intentions, he certainly encouraged it, not only by referring to Plato's philosophy but also by maintaining that some "good" or "truth" is the datum from which an Ought can be derived. This seems to imply that validity is not identical with an Ought, but is, after all, some kind of being.

2.3.2 The Baden School: Wilhelm Windelband and Heinrich Rickert

Normativism figures prominently in parts of neo-Kantian philosophy. The term 'neo-Kantianism' is not used here to denote a philosophical theory which somehow attempts to reconstruct or incorporate theorems from Kant's writings; rather, it specifically denotes a philosophical movement which dominated German philosophy between approximately 1870 and 1920, peaking at around 1900. It is characterized by two notorious slogans: '*Zurück zu Kant*' (back to Kant),[8] and '*Kant verstehen heißt über ihn hinausgehen*' (to understand Kant is to go beyond him) (Windelband 1907: IV). They express the lowest common denominator of neo-Kantianism: On the one hand, philosophy must, after decades of confusion and decay, be reformed by returning to Kant's philosophy; on the other hand, Kant's philosophy itself is not thought through in all its parts, so it needs to be complemented and improved.

Most neo-Kantians are antirealists – more so than Kant himself. For them, the objective world is not given independently of cognition; rather, it is 'constituted' by it, and they do not assign any function to the notion of a thing-in-itself.[9] It is not ontology but epistemology that is at the centre of most neo-Kantian philosophies. Accordingly, the notion of 'judgment' is one of their most fundamental elements: It is the basic unit of cognition. By comparison, the sphere of sensibility or intuition is notoriously neglected by most neo-Kantians.

There are two main schools of neo-Kantianism: the Marburg school, and the Baden school. The Marburg school, represented principally by Hermann Cohen and Paul Natorp, holds transcendental philosophy in a Kantian vein to be a theory of the exact sciences. It accepts the judgments of the culturally established and successfully operating natural sciences as a 'given' fact and critically explores the conditions of their possibility – this is the Marburg version of the 'transcendental method.' It has been aptly termed "a method-critical theory of science with extended policing powers" (Hoeschen 1999: 113). This brand of neo-Kantianism is of great importance for the further development of philosophy. It influenced logical positivism and analytical philosophy; tying philosophy to a comprehensive sociocultural practice possibly had an impact on Husserl's concept of *Lebenswelt*, and even on

---

[8] Otto Liebmann enthusiastically ended each chapter of his influential book *Kant und die Epigonen* (Schober: Stuttgart, 1865) with this slogan.

[9] See Windelband's harsh dictum: "From the standpoint of epistemology, the thing-in-itself is a completely meaningless and useless, confusing and annoying fiction" (quoted in Beiser 2014: 524).

Wittgenstein's later concept of *Lebensform*. And it is highly important for the self-conception of the Pure Theory, being responsible for Kelsen's presenting it as a theory of legal dogmatics, performing a presuppositional analysis.[10] The theory of the basic norm makes sense only when seen as an outcome of applying Cohen's 'transcendental method.' Yet the Marburg school is of no significance for the development of normativism, so it can be disregarded in the present context. The Baden school, on the other hand, represented mainly by Wilhelm Windelband and Heinrich Rickert, explicitly defines philosophy as a theory of 'values' in the wake of Lotze, thus giving it a normativist twist.

In a way, both schools of thought defended philosophy, in different ways, against the naturalist menace of being 'swallowed up' by the expanding empirical sciences: the Baden school, by demarcating an irreducible sphere of normative validity, and the Marburg school, by lifting philosophy onto a meta-level vis-à-vis the sciences.

2.3.2.1 Wilhelm Windelband

Wilhelm Windelband (1848–1915), the founder of the Baden school, was tutored by Lotze when writing his thesis on 'certainty,' which was published in 1870. He started as a historian of philosophy and never wrote a monograph containing his philosophical thoughts in a systematic way. His views are mainly contained somewhat rhapsodically in a collection of essays titled *Präludien* (Preludes).

Windelband follows Kant in maintaining that metaphysics must dissolve into epistemology, and that normativism must rule epistemology. In fact, he is a lot more explicit regarding these points. He takes Kantian philosophy to focus on the question how reference to objects is possible, and he takes Kant's answer to be that knowledge is not brought about by the correspondence of a representation with an object, but by the cognizing act being in accordance with the rules guiding the way representations have to be related to each other; for Windelband, Kant replaced the concept of object with that of a rule (Windelband 1907: 157, 160).[11] (The terms '*Regel*' [rule] and '*Norm*' [norm] are used by Windelband interchangeably.[12]) Truth is normativity of thinking; it lies in thinking's compliance with valid norms – the Lotzean origin of Windelband's philosophy is obvious. Likewise, his anti-psychologism: He maintains that "representations come and go, and psychology may explain how this comes about: philosophy analyses their value from the critical standpoint of truth" (Windelband 1907: 48, my translation).

---

[10] On this status, see Heidemann 2020: 81–98. [11] On this topic, see further Beiser 2014: 497.
[12] Cf. Beiser 2014: 497.

'Critical' (i.e. Kantian) philosophy, accordingly, boils down to a science of necessary and universally valid valuations (Windelband 1907: 49). However, Windelband is not quite clear on the problem of how to justify the rules guiding cognition and the 'basic norms' or axioms of the three disciplines of philosophy – science, ethics, and aesthetics (whose basic norms are, respectively, truth, goodness, and beauty; they apparently are values in a Lotzean sense and take the place of the Kantian 'thing-in-itself'). He seems to have different strategies.[13] On the one hand, he adopts the approach of the Marburg school of neo-Kantianism in considering philosophy as a theory of science (Windelband 1907: 42); 'science' in this sense being regarded as a successful and sociocultural established practice with a claim to objectivity. Taking science as 'given,' it follows that both the basic norms of cognition and the rules guiding cognition can be extracted (though not justified) by analyzing scientific practice. On the other hand, Windelband adopts a teleological and hypothetical approach: The rules for guiding cognition are (only) valid for anyone who aims at the basic values of truth, goodness, or beauty. In an early text, he further maintains that these values are a necessary consequence of the unity of self-consciousness (Windelband 1874: 90)[14] (which sounds both Kantian and convincing; Windelband possibly later eliminated this thesis in order to purge his theory from any seemingly psychologist elements). In yet another context, he maintains that the basic values can be derived as presuppositions of the 'normal consciousness' (*Normalbewusstsein*) (Windelband 1907: 67–9), thus exploiting, in a bit doubtful manner, the ambivalence of the term 'normal,' meaning both 'average' and 'according to norms'.

It is noteworthy that normativity seems to be important for Windelband only in connection with the analysis of cognition; the moral Ought does not play any important part in his philosophy. While it seems an accident that Lotze did not write a systematic text on ethics, it seems to be part of Windelband's program that he neglects this domain. Just one paper from *Präludien* deals with the moral Ought, and, without elaborating the difference between moral and cognitive normativity, Windelband simply expounds his position that the fundamental moral Ought is a principle even more formal than Kant's categorical imperative; it is the rule that one ought to do one's duty (Windelband 1907: 380–414). This can be explained, in part, by the aim of neo-Kantian philosophy to instrumentalize normativity to thwart any attempt of the natural sciences (including psychology) to usurp the domain of philosophy and the humanities, partly through the insight that philosophy was not able to yield specific 'moral content' anyway.

---

[13] Cf. Beiser 2014: 506–7.   [14] See further Köhnke 1993: 361.

One further trait of Windelband's theory is important for normativism. He distinguishes a "critical" from a "genetical" method. This distinction is based on Kant's differentiation between *quaestio facti* and *quaestio juris,* mentioned in Section 2.2.2. It concerns the method of philosophy, seen as a theory of validity of axioms. The genetic method looks into the origins of these axioms by employing the methods of empirical sciences; it is based on psychology and cultural history. But employing the genetic method can never answer the question why an axiom *is* valid, it can only yield an answer to the question why an axiom is *taken* to be valid; the axioms are, for this method, "factual ways of conceiving something [*Auffassungsweisen*], which took shape during the development of human ideas, feelings, and volitions" (Windelband 1907: 328, my translation). By contrast, the critical method takes these axioms, "no matter how far they are factually recognized, to be norms which are valid under the presuppositions that thinking aims at being true, willing aims at being good, and feeling aims at appreciating beauty" (Windelband 1907: 328, my translation). It is the only true philosophical method. Accordingly, philosophy's task is it to make explicit, using the critical method, the norms necessarily followed when pursuing the aims of finding out what is true, good, and beautiful – like his teacher Lotze, Windelband combines a normative approach with a teleological conception.

2.3.2.2 Heinrich Rickert

Heinrich Rickert (1863–1936), in turn, wrote his thesis under the supervision of Windelband, so that he is in several respects the philosophical 'grandson' of Lotze. His theory can be regarded as a systematic development of Windelband's philosophy. From the beginning, he is not concerned with ethics or practical philosophy, but strives to dissolve metaphysics into epistemology, and epistemology into a philosophy of values (*Wertphilosophie*).

Rickert is probably best known for elaborating Windelband's distinction between nomothetic disciplines, which concentrate on general laws, and idiographic disciplines, which examine particular events in the light of certain values, by distinguishing natural sciences from cultural sciences. This theorem strongly influenced Gustav Radbruch (the other great legal philosopher of the German language in the first half of the twentieth century besides Kelsen) and was successful enough to provoke Kelsen to write a lengthy paper against it, *Die Rechtswissenschaft als Norm- oder als Kulturwissenschaft* ('Legal science as a science of norms, or as a science of culture'), which was published in 1916.

As far as his theoretical philosophy is concerned, Rickert advocates a strictly nonrealist position. For him, there is no objective reality that is logically prior to the sphere of judgments; reality is constituted in objective cognitive judgments. To grasp the notion of an objective judgment, according to Rickert, it is necessary to distinguish between the psychical act of judging and its meaning-content. There are two kinds of meaning-contents which might be correlated to the act of judging. The subjective or "immanent" meaning-content is "that which is inherent to the real acts of judging by virtue of their capacity" (Rickert 1921: 143). By contrast, the objective or transcendent meaning-content is something that the concrete individual performance of an act of judgment 'aims at' and which is external to it. Rickert characterizes it as follows:

> That structure which we have in mind when we are talking about the objective meaning-content is what is sometimes called the "truth" of the judgment, its content per se which is not immanent to the judging act of the subject but which must be thought of as something independent of it and attained by it, and which all of us mean and understand wherever we judge or assert something as true at all. (Rickert 1921: 143, my translation)

Such an anti-psychologist interpretation of the objective meaning-content of a judgment seems to require a Platonic 'hyper-realism'; that is, an ontology of abstract meaning-contents. But Rickert wants to avoid such a metaphysics, which is scarcely compatible with critical philosophy, and simply shifts the problem of realism to a different level. His theory strives for a third alternative beyond psychologism and Platonism. To achieve this aim, Rickert – following Lotze (Rickert 1921: 229) – employs the concepts of validity (*Geltung*), Ought (*Sollen*), and theoretical value (*theoretischer Wert*). He argues as follows: The transcendent meaning-content of a judgment is objective by being necessarily correlated to the theoretical value of truth; truth is the 'form' of this meaning-content, as it were. The theoretical value, and with it the objective meaning-content, does not exist like an object, instead, it is valid. It gives rise to an Ought, namely, a demand to think in a certain way.

Validity must not be understood as an ideal mode of being of some kind of nonsensual reality (Rickert 1921: 247); rather, it is the indefinable way in which normativity is given, and which is prior to any existence:

> [The concept of existence is not the only one] under which something can be subsumed; besides, there is the concept of value. We use this word which denotes a concept that can be defined just as little as the concept of existence, for structures that do not exist but which, nevertheless, are "something", and this can best be expressed by saying that they are *valid*. (Rickert 1921: 229–30, my translation)

Rickert argues in different ways for the case that validity has not only to be distinguished from existence, but is also prior to it; the most convincing argument runs as follows:

> [The transcendent meaning] lies ... "above" and "before" everything that is existing and cannot be captured by any ontology. This simply follows from the fact that any recognition "that something exists", presupposes the meaning inherent to the sentence, that something exists, no matter whether it is a physical or a psychical, a real or an ideal, a sensual or supersensual, a given or an inferred existing. If the meaning of the existential sentence is not true, then nothing exists at all. Therefore, the meaning cannot be part of the things existing, it must be prior to it. (Rickert 1921: 229, my translation)

An object x exists only insofar as there is an objective meaning-content of a judgment (so that a sentence expressing the judgment is true), which affirms the existence of x. Therefore, the validity of the objective meaning-content is a necessary logical presupposition of any existence.

Once you accept its premises, the argument seems to be sound. It establishes, at least for transcendental idealism, the primacy of Ought, or value, over Is. The problem with it is that Rickert is not able to balance the relation between the immanent and the transcendent meaning-content in a satisfactory manner. This matter deserves a digression. On the one hand, this problem is not only the crux of neo-Kantian *Wertphilosophie*, its descendants also haunt parts of contemporary philosophy. On the other hand, Kelsen refers to it in some crucial passages when explaining the notions of Ought and, especially, validity (see Section 3.2.4.3 below). It can best be assessed by examining Husserl's (because he is the main protagonist of antipsychologism), Windelband's, and Rickert's attempts to answer the question whether and how logical laws and cognitive content might be regarded as being normative. Philosophically, it is the most thrilling aspect of 'old-school' normativism.

2.3.3 Digression: Immanence and Transcendence, Norm and Value

Edmund Husserl (1859–1938), one of the main protagonists of anti-psychologism, seems to worry that taking logical principles to be 'prescriptive' for the acts of a factually existing subject may impair their absolute character and necessarily drag them back into the mire of psychologism. Therefore, he distinguishes a 'pure' logic, which is not a normative but a theoretical discipline, from an 'applied' logic, which determines how we ought to think. Logics, understood as a set of norms for thinking, seems to belong to a strange intermediate region between psychological acts and the transcendent sphere of pure logics, while the latter does not contain any normative Ought. Husserl admits that the laws of pure logic might, like every general truth, serve as "a general norm for judging correctly." But by their own nature, they are not normative, but theoretical truths, and as such they can serve for regulating the activity of judging just as much as truths from any other disciplines. ... The anti-psychologists erred in taking the regulation of cognition as the essence of the laws of logic. ... It was overlooked that the so-called logical principles as such are not norms, but may be used as norms. With respect to this function we got used to speaking of laws of thinking, and so it seemed as if these laws had a psychological content, and as if the difference to the so-called laws of psychology was just that they regulate, while the other laws of psychology do not. On the other hand, the psychologists erred. ... It is a matter of course that every general truth, be it of psychology or not, founds a rule of correct judging; and thus not only the possibility, but the existence of rules for judging is confirmed, which are not founded in psychology. (Husserl 1900: 157, my translation)

Windelband holds in a similar way that

the pure logic or logic in the narrow sense is usually defined as the theory of the forms of thinking. But this has to be specified; it is concerned with the forms of correct thinking, which are a selection from the psychologically possible forms of moves of mental representations. Logic does not teach how we really think, but how we ought to think, if we want to think correctly. ... One has to keep in mind, however that the validity of these forms has, in the end, to be totally independent from the quest for knowledge of an empirical and especially the human consciousness. ... From this, a fundamental duality of all logical laws follows: On the one hand, they are rules for empirical consciousness which all thinking that is directed toward truth should comply with; on the other hand, their inner and autonomous meaning and being is quite independent from the question whether there are factual mental processes of representing which conform to them. The former might be called their validity in itself [Geltung an sich], the latter their validity for us [Geltung für uns]; where "us" does not just mean us human beings, but all individual subjects who – like us – distinguish, in their representations, between true and false, correct and incorrect. Seen from "us," logic is an "Ought" – but this Ought must be grounded in something whose validity subsists in itself, and which turns into a norm or Ought only if it is related to a consciousness capable of erring. (Windelband 1912: 17–18, my translation)

Finally, Rickert devotes an almost book-length text (Rickert 1909) to showing – in a manner comparable to that of Windelband – that although normativity is a fundamental element of cognition, it is not simply by applying norms for cognition that the correctness of judgments comes about. According to Rickert, there are two different ways for cognitive theory to proceed. On the one hand, it is possible to start at the psychical act of judging and explore the normative rules necessarily involved in it. Rickert calls this procedure the "transcendental-psychological way." The problem with it is that its results are by necessity relative to the act of judging; so that the norms recognized in the act of judging are still somehow part of the psychological sphere – or so Rickert holds. Therefore, the transcendental-psychological way has to be complemented by a "transcendental-logical" way or method. The transcendental-logical method does not start with the psychological act of judging, but with the transcendent sphere of values from which the norms for judging are derived. The reason, for Rickert, is that thinking must have an object which is not part of it, but external to it; otherwise thinking would not have an object at all, because an object must offer "resistance" to cognition.

Characteristic of the conceptions of Windelband and Rickert is that, in order to ward off psychologism (and its associates, relativism and naturalism), they think it necessary not to see Ought-normativity as basic, but to ground it in something more abstract. In order for the norms of thinking not to be part of the psychological sphere, they have to be derived not as a presupposition of the act of thinking, but from values which rest in themselves, detached from human affairs. And thus, though they fly the flag of transcendental idealism (and deny a knowledge-independent existence of everyday objects), in the end Windelband and Rickert run danger of falling prey to hyper-realism, that is, of endorsing the thesis that there are transcendent, knowledge-independent, values.

The way Rickert tries to deal with this consequence and to find a point where the transcendent value and the immanent norm or Ought might have contact, is remarkable for its meandering. The first step is to remove the transcendent value from the realm of existing objects. This is made possible, as shown in Section 2.3.2.2, by introducing the notion of 'validity.' The second step is to determine some graspable thing, which is not reducible to a psychical entity and which, in a way, embodies the transcendent value. This graspable object, for Rickert, is the true "sentence," understood as a series of signs (Rickert 1909: 194). Its meaning is "transcendent," independent of cognitive acts, and has to be distinguished from the "immanent" subjective meaning of these acts. Like Frege, Rickert calls this objective meaning a "thought" (*Gedanke*) (Rickert 1909: 196). It is logically prior to any existence, because – as was shown in Section 2.3.2.2 – for Rickert, existence presupposes the validity of an objective-meaning content. Being logically prior to existence, the true thought can only be made sense of as a "theoretical value," and, accordingly, the task of cognitive theory is to determine its presuppositions (Rickert 1909: 207).

There is an obvious objection to this argumentation: Why should it be possible to get at the transcendent meaning by simply connecting it to the empirical object of a 'sentence,' to a series of signs? After all, the meaning of a sentence is accessible only via the psychical act of 'understanding' it. So,

either the transcendent meaning is identical with the immanent meaning of an
act of understanding a true sentence, or it is, again, inaccessible.

Rickert tries to answer this objection, first, by maintaining vaguely that
transcendental psychology might bridge the gap; "we," as practically free
beings, might autonomously recognize "the Ought for its own sake, and the
value for its own sake." Only as practically free beings might we take posses-
sion of the realm of transcendent values (Rickert 1909: 222). But just a few
sentences later he seems to capitulate and to admit the validity of the objection:

> Nevertheless, there might still be concerns about the worth of the transcen-
> dental-psychological analysis, especially as regards its ability to bridge the
> gap between the world of theoretical values and the psychical acts of think-
> ing. To support these doubts, a very radical argument may be brought forward
> that at this point the theory of cognition hits upon a problem which cannot be
> solved at all. Meaning and being, value and reality, transcendence and
> immanence conceptually exclude each other. Philosophy cannot overcome
> this dualism, not even by introducing the conception of autonomously recog-
> nising the values. (Rickert 1909: 222, my translation)

However, in the passage following this concession, Rickert maintains that
one should not give up over this problem. The seeming dualism of immanence
and transcendence is just

> the necessary product of any reflection about cognition. We have cognition,
> and grasp the truth at the same time. There is an immediacy of the unity of
> meaning and being which is "experienced". But, alas, by asserting that "we"
> have and experience this "unity" we must destroy this immediate unity and
> divide it into a real cognitive act and its non-real object. This division is
> necessarily connected with the concept of cognition. We cannot even say that
> there is this unity, because that would be cognition of the unity as unity, which
> is impossible. The unity cannot be thought, it can only be experienced.
> (Rickert 1909: 223–4, my translation)

This is no true solution. If the unity of immanence and transcendence is to be
proved by an unreflected "experience" of this unity in an act of cognition, then
transcendence is dependent on immanence. However the problem of the relation
between the immanent and the transcendent aspects of normativity might be
solved, it is certainly not by pointing to the dichotomy of immanent norm and
transcendent value.[15] As meritorious as Lotze's idea was, of demarcating the
domain of cognition, which cannot be 'naturalized,' by introducing the notion

---

[15] The problem of the relation between immanence and transcendence troubles even so late
a descendant of neo-Kantianism as Jürgen Habermas. In *Wahrheit und Rechtfertigung* he holds
that "it is the aim of all justification to discover a truth which is independent of any justification"
(Habermas 1999: 53, my translation). This sentence is paradoxical not only at first sight.

of validity, it was not really helpful to his successors that he conceptualized those elements to which validity might be attributed as transcendent and object-like. A more plausible solution, faintly hinted at in the last Rickert quote above, would be to go back to the notion of 'implicit normativity,' which can be found – as was shown in Section 2.2.2 – in Kant's philosophy and which is prominent in Wittgenstein's conception of rule-following in the *Philosophical Investigations*.

2.4 Summary

The genesis of normativism as outlined in this section might be summarized as follows: Hume was the first major philosopher to make the dualism of Is and Ought explicit, taking the Ought to be a matter of moral, religious, or political propositions and holding Ought-sentences not to be objective. Kant took the moral Ought to be expressive of practical reason (and, therefore, to be object-ive). Although he explicitly dealt only with the moral Ought in an elaborate way, there is a 'theoretical' Ought (recognized in any act of judging) in Kant's theory as well. Lotze gave an ontological touch to this theoretical Ought by taking a truth to be the "content of cogitation" which is valid and from which an Ought, or rules demanding that a subject should think in a certain way, can be derived. This interpretation was taken up by Windelband in order to make the normativ-ity of values the basic philosophical element and to forestall any psychologistic explanation of cognition (while neglecting the moral or practical Ought). Rickert systematized and radicalized Windelband's approach by distinguishing between the Ought directed at the judging person's subjectivity and the even more fundamental value of truth which is valid independent of any subjectivity. His theory, however, hit upon new problems by distinguishing between a "transcendent" Ought, embodied by values independent of any human cogni-tion, and an "immanent" Ought, embodied by norms directing cognition which somehow emanate from the transcendent Ought.

3 Hans Kelsen's Normativism

Section 2 outlined the philosophical setting concerning normativism when Kelsen entered the stage. It was the outcome of a deep, highly sophisticated, multifaceted and not always commonsensical discussion over more than a century.

Now, especially due to the writings of Stanley L. Paulson,[16] it is largely accepted that Kelsen's legal-theoretical writings must be assigned different phases to avoid grave inconsistencies and to do justice to their philosophical

---

[16] See especially Paulson 1990; see further Kubeš 1980.

fundamentals. According to my count, there are four different phases, distinguishable by the philosophical basis of the writings assigned to them, and their consequences (cf. Heidemann 2007). The first phase covers Kelsen's habilitation thesis, *Hauptprobleme der Staatsrechtslehre* (*Main Problems of the Theory of State Law*) from 1911, and some subsequent shorter texts. In the writings of this period, there are a lot of anticipations of theorems of what was later called "Pure Theory of Law," but there is no coherent philosophical or epistemological underpinning as yet. Between about 1916 and 1935, Kelsen develops most of the special tenets of the Pure Theory in full and grounds them in a specific neo-Kantian epistemology. From around 1940 until 1960, he does without any explicit philosophical foundation for his theory but relies on a rather naive cognitive realism according to which the legal norm is an entity 'given' to cognition; after 1960 he introduces a rather heterogeneous jumble of philosophical conceptions into his theory – especially from linguistic philosophy –and couples them with a strict will-theory of norms.[17]

3.1 The First Phase: Juristic Constructivism

With his first major publication,[18] *Hauptprobleme der Staatsrechtslehre*, Kelsen did not emerge as a legal philosopher: He was trained as a jurist, and he understood his text in the first instance as a methodology of legal dogmatics. Its aim is to answer "preliminary questions" for any legal cognition (Kelsen 1911: III). Kelsen presupposes as fact that there is an autonomous legal cognition – that is, a cognition which is neither sociological nor ethical – in which positive[19] law is viewed as something that is objective and normative (Kelsen 1911: VI, 44)[20], namely, the cognition of practical jurists and legal dogmatists. It is reconstructed from the internal perspective; Kelsen aims to uncover its tacit presuppositions and to criticize its constructions (Kelsen 1911: V).

The methodological assumption underlying this enterprise is the distinction between an explicative view, employed by causal sciences, and a normative view, employed by legal science (that is, legal dogmatics). Both views exclude

---

[17] For a detailed depiction of the genesis of Kelsen's normativism, see Heidemann 1997.

[18] He published a book on Dante's theory of state six years earlier (Hans Kelsen, *Die Staatslehre des Dante Alighieri*, *Wiener Staatswissenschaftliche Studien*, series 6, vol. 3 [1905]), but it does not contain any traces of the later Pure Theory. Kelsen himself regarded it as "a student's unoriginal effort" (see Kelsen 2006: 37).

[19] Kelsen takes for granted that the term 'law' covers exclusively the positive law, cf. Kelsen 1911: 367.

[20] The 'normative perspective' of legal dogmatics is, for Kelsen, as much a postulate as a reality. Calling legal dogmatics a 'normative' discipline only means that norms are its subject matter; it does not mean that it posits norms (Kelsen 1911: VI–VII).

each other and must not be blended in one and the same science (Kelsen 1911: 6). Therefore, Kelsen aims at restricting juristic construction by eliminating from it any elements alien to the normative view – especially arguments from psychology or sociology – in order to get at a logically closed system of purely juridical fundamental concepts (Kelsen 1911: XI).

This alone, however, would not have been a radical innovation of contemporary conceptions of law and state. In fact, Kelsen himself – in a later text, *Allgemeine Staatslehre* (1925) – saw his theory in the positivistic tradition of Gerber and Laband, who applied *Begriffsjurisprudenz* (conceptual jurisprudence) to state law (Kelsen 1925: VII). And stressing the normativity of law was not new either; Kelsen was preceded, among others, by Georg Jellinek who was closely related to the Baden school of neo-Kantianism. Kelsen had attended his seminars at Heidelberg.

So what was actually new about Kelsen's approach? On the one hand, it was the radicality with which he defined the dualism of Is and Ought and attempted to exclude any 'Is-elements' from law. On the other hand, it was his 'semi-reductionism' concerning legal concepts, that is, his attempt to construct these concepts from the one central normative element of law, the *Rechtssatz*.

3.1.1 The Dualism of Is and Ought and the Teleological Perspective

The basis of the distinction between the explicative and the normative point of view is the dualism between Is and Ought. Accordingly, Kelsen emphasizes the importance of separating these elements. He does not develop a fully fledged argument; instead, Kelsen points to diverse lesser known or nonphilosophical writers, like Georg Simmel and Arnold Kitz (Kelsen 1911: 7–8), or Julius Kirchmann (Kelsen 1911: 19 fn.). The dualism is described in several different ways:

(1)   According to an epistemological explanation, Is and Ought are exclusive and comprehensive *Denkbestimmungen* (determinants of thought), original categories which cannot be derived from anything else (Kelsen 1911: 7). The Ought is pure form; it is not necessarily connected with any content (Kelsen 1911: 10). It is a mode of thinking, like future, simple past, subjunctive, or optative (Kelsen 1911: 7–8).

(2)   According to an ontological explanation, Is and Ought are, rather, expressive of "two separate worlds" (Kelsen 1911: 8). By constituting natural law and norm, respectively, they constitute "reality" (understood as bodily or psychical events), on the one hand, and "ideality," on the other.

(3)   According to a "formal-logical" explanation, the mutual independence of Is and Ought manifests itself in the fact that, logically, an Ought can be justified only by pointing to another Ought; and an Is can only be justified by pointing to another Is. The chain of justification inside the respective spheres is infinite; and it is just a "psychological need of limitation" which wants to ground the Ought-chain on an Is, and the Is-chain on an Ought (Kelsen 1911: 9).

It is a special feature of Kelsen's version of the Is–Ought dualism that he not only maintains that an Ought cannot be derived from an Is; he also holds that an Is cannot be derived from an Ought. And there is a relativization of the dichotomy. In a prominent passage in the foreword to the *Hauptprobleme*, Kelsen writes that the dualism of Is and Ought emanates from a comprehensive dualistic world view according to which "I and world, soul and body, subject and object, form and content" are unbridgeably separated. At the same time, he relativizes the dualism by holding that the choice between such a dualistic view and a monistic view is a matter of *Weltanschauung* (Kelsen 1911: 5–6).

A further candidate (besides Is and Ought) for a fundamental perspective is dismissed by Kelsen rather easily: the teleological view. As was shown in Sections 2.3.1 and 2.3.2 teleology was a dominant factor both in Lotze's philosophy and in the philosophy of the Baden school, where norms directed at human acting and thinking are derived from abstract values which are the *telos* of acting and thinking. Besides, teleological thinking dominated parts of the juristic discourse. According to Kelsen, however, the teleological view is a special case of the explicative view. It is directed at understanding occurrences, especially human acts, by the "means–end-scheme." And the means–end-scheme is just an application of the causal scheme: An end can only be achieved by some means if this means can work as a cause to bring about the end as its effect. Although it does not follow, according to Kelsen, that the teleological view can be reduced to the causal view; they just offer different perspectives of the same principle which governs the explicative way of cognition: the principle of sufficient reason (Kelsen 1911: 57–63).

3.1.2 Relations between Is and Ought

Even though it is not possible to deduce an Ought from an Is, or an Is from an Ought, there are several relations between them.

(1)   Both the ways an Ought comes into existence and is 'destroyed' are part of the sphere of Is (Kelsen 1911: 10). An example of this phenomenon is Jellinek's formula of the "normative force of the factual," according to which custom can produce a consciousness of Ought (Kelsen 1911: 9). However, it is not possible

to answer the question why something ought to be done, by pointing to custom or psychical processes or something else from the factual sphere (Kelsen 1911: 9, 71).

(2) Is and Ought are related insofar as the Ought "aims"at an Is. It "wants to bring about" changes in the sphere of Is. Accordingly, the "demands of the Ought" (*Sollanforderungen*) are motives for the will, and these demands are complied with by the ones they are directed at, or they can be "applied" by other individuals (Kelsen 1911: 14).

(3) There is a close relation between the Ought and the will. Willing is a factual psychical process belonging to the sphere of Is. It is relevant to the Ought in two different ways: as the will of somebody who posits an Ought-demand, and as the will of somebody who the Ought-demand is directed at. In both cases, the Ought must be strictly separated from the act of will; for it is possible that the process of willing has terminated while the Ought is still valid (Kelsen 1911: 10–11). Kelsen, however, is not clear on the point whether there can be an Ought without any volitional procedure founding it.[21]

(4) Kelsen holds that Is and Ought can have a content which is "comparable" (Kelsen 1911: 69); this content or point of reference of both Is and Ought is a "notion" (*Vorstellung*) (Kelsen 1911: 7). But he also maintains that the relation between Is and Ought is a relation between content and form (Kelsen 1911: 10); this would mean that the content of an Ought is an Is.

(5) Norms, the units of Ought, exist in reality by evoking a certain behavior. A norm is "efficacious" if it is complied with, that is, if it really determines the will of the individual subjected to the norm. A norm is "applied" if it is used as a scheme of evaluation for some factual act as being, or not being, in accordance with the norm. A secondary function of any norm is that it demands that an act which is in accordance with it is approved, and that an act which is not in accordance with it is disapproved, so that approval/disapproval are secondary ways of applying a norm (Kelsen 1911: 14–17).

3.1.3 Law of Nature and Norm; Value and Duty

Like Kant, Lotze, and the neo-Kantians, Kelsen does not give a detailed definition of 'norm' in this early phase and, like them, he juxtaposes norm and law of nature. A law of nature describes and explains reality, that is, factual processes (Kelsen 1911: 6). The explanatory function is due to the causal principle which is the basis of any natural science. Every natural law is "a judgment which

---

[21] See Kelsen 1911: 67, on the one hand and Kelsen 1911: VI, on the other.

comprehends a process as a necessary consequence of another process in a group of sequences of the same kind, thus explaining it" (Kelsen 1911: 5, my translation). By contrast, norms are rules which constitute an Ought. Kelsen lists diverse types of norms, namely, moral and legal norms, logical norms, and grammatical and aesthetic rules (Kelsen 1911: 5).

Natural laws aim at explaining something which is given, while norms aim at bringing about something which is not yet given (Kelsen 1911: 14). The causal principle is not valid in the sphere of norms. Facts are relevant for norms not by being real; rather, as content of norms, they are part of the ideal sphere (Kelsen 1911: 6). And any human act is subject to natural laws, but not every human act is regulated by norms (Kelsen 1911: 13).

The most important normative element for Lotze and the neo-Kantians of the Baden school was the 'value,' whose validity removed it far away from any human willing or thinking. Not so for Kelsen. For him, the norm is the fundamental Ought-element. Values in an objective sense are a function of norms; a judgment stating a value concerns the relation between a fact or an individual and a norm. The validity of a norm is not derived from some transcendent value; a norm is valid because it contains an objective Ought (Kelsen 1911: 14), that is, because it ought to be complied with or applied. Whether the norm has any effects in the sphere of factuality or not (its efficacy) is of no avail to its validity (Kelsen 1911: 352).

Finally, a duty is not the same as a norm, either. The objective norm contains an abstract general ought, while the duty is a concrete individual Ought directed at someone subjected to the norm.[22]

Any norm is a structure of norm-subject and norm-object. In the formula 'x ought to (do) a,' x is norm-subject and a is norm-object (which might be an act or some state of affairs)[23]. Norm-subject and norm-object do not exist as parts of the factual world but as ideal reference points of the Ought, which relates them to each other in the norm. Accordingly, there need not be any causal relation between them, and the norm-subject is not a physical human being, but a 'person'; so a person is nothing but an ideally constructed reference point of the Ought (Kelsen 1911: 72–4).

Kelsen labels the relation between norm-subject and norm-object somewhat contra-intuitively as '*Zurechnung*' (imputation); a term which will become important especially in his neo-Kantian phase. It stays opaque. Kelsen uses

---

[22] See the extensive discussion in Kelsen 1911: 313–46.

[23] Although he was one of the first legal theorists to introduce formulas for describing legal relations (cf. Kelsen 1925: 49), Kelsen does not yet use any of them in the *Hauptprobleme*. He defines the norm-subject as "*dasjenige, was soll*" (the one who ought to do something) and the norm-object as "*dasjenige, was gesollt wird*" (that which ought to be done); Kelsen 1911: 71–2.

this term not only to denominate the relation between the abstract elements *inside the norm*, but also to denote the relation between certain elements of *factual reality*, a human being and some factual act or process, which are related as the result of an application of the norm (Kelsen 1911: 72). The difference can be illustrated as follows: Originally, imputation connects 'help the needy' with 'everybody' in the norm 'Everybody ought to help the needy'; but it also connects the factual process of helping a needy human being with the one who is helping him. This ambiguity will accompany the notion of *Zurechnung* in Kelsen's later phases.

3.1.4 The Normative Domain of Law

Normativism in law was provisionally defined in Section 1 as the view that law is exclusively a system of (normative) rules which are objective, impersonal, and independent of any factuality. Accordingly, for Kelsen, the law consists of norms; and what makes his view normativistic is that it contains *nothing but* norms. It follows that every concept that is relevant for law must be derived from a legal norm, its parts, or the set of all legal norms. It is a construction; that is why Stanley L. Paulson's description of this phase of Kelsen's writings as "critical constructivism" (Paulson 1990: 24–8) is appropriate.

3.1.4.1 The Legal Norm

The legal norm differs from the moral norm insofar as the latter is posited "autonomously," that is, by the norm-subject him-/herself (Kelsen 1911: 21–2, 41), while the former is posited "heteronomously," that is, by somebody else (Kelsen 1911: 36–7). Kelsen identifies the legal norm with the *Rechtssatz* (Kelsen 1911: 3) – a hypothetical judgment (in a logical sense) about the will of the state. It is not "given" to legal dogmatics; rather, it has to be put together by lawyers from the fragmented empirical material supplied by the legislative procedure; so it is, on a different level, a "construction," as well. The hypothetical judgment is the "logical" or "ideal" form of the legal norm. This further distinguishes the legal norm from the moral norm, which is an imperative (Kelsen 1911: 236–7).

Every *Rechtssatz* can be formulated as "Under conditions c, the state wants to act in the way a" (Kelsen 1911: 207, 211–12). Like the norm in general, it is a rule of imputation. But while the norm in general relates to a certain act or state of affairs for a norm-subject as something which she ought to do or bring about, the *Rechtssatz* is a law imputing an act to the state as being willed by it. The *Rechtssatz* in a wider sense may impute any act to the state; in a narrow sense it imputes coercion to the state – the state not being a given entity, but a unifying construct.

This definition of the legal norm raises questions: On the one hand, the formulation of the *Rechtssatz* seems to be a pure stipulation; on the other hand, the Ought seems to be lost somehow – at least it does not appear in the formula. With regard to the first point, Kelsen argues that law is necessarily the will of the state; but a will cannot be directed at somebody else's behavior, which can only be wished for; so the will of the state can only be directed at 'its own' behavior. Regarding the second point, Kelsen holds that the Ought is somehow connected with the hypothetical judgment about the will of the state, but he does not settle in a satisfactory way how this connection might be conceived. The most relevant passage runs as follows:

> If the norm drapes itself in the form of a judgment, then it raises a general claim to truth, and it repeats itself in anybody who hears it, like any judgment. As a judgment, the proposition: If somebody steals, then the state wills to commit him to prison, is as true and universally – i.e. for any reasonable being – valid as the proposition: The state is powerful, or: The horse is a mammal. But this logical universal validity is of no consequence for the validity of the norm posited together with the judgment. (Kelsen 1911: 259, my translation)

This explanation is, at best, ambiguous: On the one hand, the judgment is the "form" of the norm; on the other, there is a difference between the logical validity of the hypothetical judgment of the *Rechtssatz* and the validity of the Ought, which is somehow connected to the judgment. And it almost seems as if the norm is "posited" together with the judgment. This does not go together well.

The source of the validity of a single legal norm is, in this early phase, tabooed by Kelsen. He maintains that, for legal dogmatics, it is not permissible to ask why a single norm is valid because this question concerns its own presuppositions. To ask it would mean, for the jurist, "to saw off the bough he is sitting on" (Kelsen 1911: 353). To illustrate the analogous problem of 'Is-science' to ascertain a final ground of the world, Kelsen cites Franz Grillparzer: "*Geläng' es mir, des Weltalls Grund, / somit auch meinen auszusagen, / so könnt' ich auch zur selben Stund' / mich selbst auf meinen Armen tragen*" (Should I succeed the reason to name / of the universe, and, thus, mine own, / I could – it would be just the same – / carry myself on my arms alone) (Kelsen 1911: 466).

This quaintly expressed 'taboo' is a congenial placeholder for the basic norm, which will be introduced only in the next phase.

3.1.4.2 The Construction of Legal Concepts

The second ingredient of Kelsen's normativism is that *every* element of the law, every legal concept, must be shown to be a construction based on legal norms.

The will of the state – or the state as a person, which is nothing else but this will – is not an empirical entity; it exists just as a "point of imputation" which is constituted by the *Rechtssätze*. It is something quite different from the empirical will which might be part of the legislative procedures but which is, inside the law, irrelevant. The same applies to the concepts of will and person in general: Both elements only exist as reference points, that is, as constructed points of the imputation of acts by legal norms (Kelsen 1911: 145–6). The concepts of "duty" and "(subjective) right" can be shown to be constructions from the *Rechtssatz* as well: A duty of the state is the result of a "subjectification" of the *Rechtssatz* (this procedure is not further explained by Kelsen) (Kelsen 1911: 435). Besides, there is a duty for a citizen if the *Rechtssatz* says that, under certain conditions, the state wants the citizen to be sanctioned (Kelsen 1911: 447). And somebody has a right to a certain act of somebody else if he is able to 'trigger' the state's will to sanction this somebody else in case he omits this act (Kelsen 1911: 618–29).

3.2 Neo-Kantian Transcendental Idealism

The second phase of the Pure Theory, lasting from approximately 1920 to 1935, is its heyday. Not only does it offer the most sophisticated theory of legal cognition Kelsen ever advocated, it is also his most productive period. Between 1920 and 1934 Kelsen published four monographs: *Das Problem der Souveränität und die Theorie des Völkerrechts* (*The Problem of Sovereignty and the Theory of International Law*, 1920); *Der soziologische und der juristische Staatsbegriff* (*The Sociological and the Legal Concept of State*, 1922); *Allgemeine Staatslehre* (*General Theory of State*, 1925); and *Reine Rechtslehre* (*Pure Theory of Law*, 1934). He also wrote numerous longer treatises which were published in journals or as brochures; the most important ones are *Die Grundlagen der Naturrechtslehre und des Rechtspositivismus* (*The Foundations of the Natural Law Doctrine and Legal Positivism*, 1928), and a book-length text dealing with the theory of Fritz Sander, *Rechtswissenschaft und Recht* (*Legal Science and Law*, 1922).

The books on sovereignty and on the concept of state, in particular, are brilliantly written and contain more elaborate arguments than almost anything Kelsen wrote after 1940; the polemical *Rechtswissenschaft und Recht* is rather chaotic and sloppily formulated, but it gives a unique glimpse into Kelsen's nascent neo-Kantianism whose final version is summarized in the Foreword to the second edition of *Hauptprobleme der Staatsrechtslehre* (1923). The short *Reine Rechtslehre* is in many respects the closing text of this phase; in concise and slightly Kafkaesque language, Kelsen gives a summary of his legal theory, stating his theses in a rather apodictic way without elaborating the foundations of his theory.

In secondary literature, it is sometimes suspected that Kelsen's neo-Kantianism is no more than a pretentious label. This is, however, only justified as far as his writings from 1940 onward are concerned. For the 1920s, there can be no doubt that Kelsen really is a true-blue neo-Kantian.

But what is neo-Kantian about Kelsen's theory in this phase? According to Kelsen himself, he was not aware of the affinities between his theory and neo-Kantianism until 1912, when he read a review of his *Hauptprobleme* in the *Kant-Studien* by Oscar Ewald (Kelsen 1998a: 15 [Kelsen 1923: XVII]). Ewald pointed specifically to his treatment of the concept of will, which he thought was "remarkably in accord" with what Cohen had advocated in his *Ethik des Reinen Willens*. And he appreciated the book as an attempt to introduce the "transcendental method" into the theory of state law. The review spurred Kelsen to focus on neo-Kantian philosophy. This had two main impacts on his theory: First, Kelsen conceived his legal theory as a neo-Kantian transcendental philosophy of law, that is, as a theory of legal science as embodied by legal dogmatics; second, Kelsen identified the legal norm with the hypothetical judgment of legal science.

3.2.1 Transcendental Idealism

Transcendental idealism is at the core of Kant's theoretical philosophy. Kelsen explains it, approvingly, as follows:

> It is impossible for cognition to play just a *passive* part in relation to its objects; it cannot be restricted to *reflecting* things somehow existing "in themselves", i.e. in a transcendent sphere. As soon as we can no longer assume objects to have a transcendent, i.e. knowledge-independent, existence, cognition has to play an *active, creative* part in relation to these objects. It is *cognition itself which creates its objects from the material given to it by the senses according to its immanent laws.* Cognition's being guided by rules guarantees the *objective validity* of its results. ... What takes the place of metaphysical speculation is the task of determining the rules guiding the process of cognition, i.e. the objective conditions of this process. (Kelsen 1928a: 62, my translation)

This is the classical (neo-)Kantian argument: It is impossible to compare a cognition of an object with the object itself; it is only possible to compare one cognition of an object with another cognition of the same object. Therefore, philosophical realism must fail as a comprehensible theory of cognition, at least as far as it involves an adequation theory of truth or cognition. Accordingly, any acceptable metaphysics is not concerned with the most fundamental elements as they might be 'in themselves'; rather, it deals with the necessary rules guiding cognition: Ontology turns into epistemology (understood as a theory of cognitive validity).

3.2.2 The Status of the Pure Theory as a Theory of Legal Science

But Kelsen's neo-Kantianism is not restricted to adopting this transcendental-idealistic conception of cognition in its classical form. As shown in Section 2.3.2, according to Cohen the object of philosophical analysis is 'given' science, that is, science successfully operating as a sociocultural practice: Traditional metaphysics, which, for Kant, dissolved into an analytic of understanding, further dissolved, for neo-Kantians who were following Cohen, into a theory of the necessary elements and presuppositions of established science.

Conceiving the Pure Theory in this way as a theory of legal science is at first glance not much of an innovation. There seem to be affinities between a 'methodology of legal dogmatics' and a 'theory of legal science.' However, the former is just a heuristic means, while a theory of science in a neo-Kantian sense takes the place of classical metaphysics; it is *prima philosophia*. What Kelsen had expounded as an unpretentious "methodology" in *Hauptprobleme*, all of a sudden becomes an ambitious equivalent to an 'ontology of law.' No wonder that he was enchanted by this outlook: "[R]eferring to the fact of science is the essential of transcendental philosophy, the only basis from which it – as a theory of scientifical experience – performs its analyses of its only possible object, the synthetic judgments of experience as science" (Kelsen 1922a: 128, my translation). It follows that the scientific judgment is "the cornerstone of transcendental philosophy, which, therefore, can only be critique of science, critique of cognition, because it is restricted to analysing the synthetic judgment" (Kelsen 1922a: 128, my translation).

The importance of adopting this conception, taking the fact of science and scientifical judgments as 'given,' can hardly be overestimated. It is responsible for the hypothetical approach of the Pure Theory (if the results of legal dogmatics as a practice are taken to be valid, then the following elements of law and their presuppositions have to be accepted), and at the same time offers an additional argument for Kelsen's relativism. Furthermore, it is expressive of Kelsen's view of the Ought which deviates from the Kantian tradition: For Kant, the Ought was not a category of understanding employed in theoretical judgments; rather, it emanated from (practical) reason. For Kelsen, there is no practical reason; the Ought *is* a category of understanding, employed in the synthetical judgments of legal science. Its status is analogous to that of the category of causality. Accordingly, legal science is not a practical, but a theoretical science.

But the Pure Theory as a theory of legal science does not only perform a presuppositional analysis of legal dogmatics; it has a 'critical' function, as well: All those elements of established legal dogmatics which are not in accordance with its presuppositions, or with the requirements any scientific practice has to meet, are eliminated (Kelsen 1992: 1 [Kelsen 1934: 1]). This function of the Pure Theory results in the 'purity thesis' which makes up Kelsen's version of the 'third feature' of normativism. The argument would run as follows: Established legal dogmatics expresses itself in normative sentences. If we take this seriously, its judgments are Ought-judgments. As Ought-judgments cannot be derived from Is-judgments, and to satisfy the scientific requirement that 'methodological syncretism' is to be avoided, legal science must consist exclusively of Ought-judgments.[24]

3.2.3 The Hypothetical Judgment as the Fundamental Cognitive Unit

While the legal norm, in *Hauptprobleme*, was necessarily connected with the *Rechtssatz*, these elements were nevertheless not identical: The validity or existence of the legal norm was different from the validity of the hypothetical judgment constructed from the legislative material given to legal dogmatics. Or so Kelsen maintained. Now, in his neo-Kantian phase, Kelsen explicitly identifies the legal norm with the hypothetical judgment of legal science; the validity of a legal norm is its validity as a cognitive judgment. A pithy formulation of this thesis can be found in *Rechtswissenschaft und Recht*:

> [Sander fails to see] that legal science may "create" its object – law as embodied by legal rules [*Rechtssätze*], by judgments – just as natural science may "create" its object, the nature of natural science, nature as a system of synthetic judgments without in the least running any danger of becoming a "source" of law. ... Though "created" by science itself, the synthetic judgments of natural science are determined by the material which they unify (therefore, they are judgments "about" [*über*] nature) just as the synthetic judgments of legal science, the legal rules, in which the material given to legal science ... is formed, formed into legal rules in the same way as the perceptual material is formed in the synthetic judgments of natural science. ... If we are inclined to qualify the acts which are

---

[24] The fight against methodological syncretism, or against the 'metabasis eis allo genos,' is a central theme for neo-Kantian anti-psychologists and for Kelsen; see Kelsen 1920: V; Kelsen 1922b: 34, 45.

the material of the legal rules as acts of will [*Willensakte*], then the legal rules as judgments "about" them have to be expressed by an Ought. In cognition, i.e. in the judgments of legal science appearing as legal rules, the willing [*Wollen*], which is objectified in the sphere of judgment, expresses itself as an Ought. Only in this sphere can we talk of law as an object of legal science. As the object of legal science, law is a system of judgments about law, just as nature as the object of natural science is a system of judgments about nature. (Kelsen 1922a: 181–2, my translation)

Accordingly, "[both the state and the law are] normative order[s], i.e. system[s] of norms which are linguistically expressed by Ought-sentences and logically in hypothetical judgments in which the condition is connected to the conse-quence by the 'Ought' (if a, then b ought to be)" (Kelsen 1922b: 75, my translation).

The above may be summarized as follows: Cognition creates its objects by synthesizing judgments. These judgments are objectively valid without corres-ponding to something 'given' to them by being in accordance with the rules that guide cognition. 'Nature' as the object of knowledge is not a conglomeration of knowledge-independent 'things,' but a system of synthetic judgments. In these judgments the category of causality is applied to perceptual material. In an analogous way, the law as the object of legal science is identical with the system of judgments created by legal science. It is not the task of legal science to 'passively' describe norms given by the legislator; rather it applies the Ought to a nonnormative substratum consisting of the legislator's acts of will (or their content), thus constituting hypothetical normative judgments which are identi-cal with the legal norms.[25]

3.2.4 Is and Ought

It was shown in Section 2 that Hume thought the dualism of Is and Ought to be one between objective analytical or empirical sentences, and subjective prac-tical sentences. Kant, by contrast, took practical sentences to be objective, and introduced normativity into epistemology, so that there was a bifurcation of the dualism of Is and Ought. The neo-Kantians concentrated on the epistemological part of the dualism, equating the theoretical Ought with a cognitive judgment's validity.

It is not easy to locate Kelsen's version of the dualism in this context. He still maintains that the reason or ground (*Grund*) for the validity of a norm can only be another norm (Kelsen 1920: 95). Besides, there is another 'formal–logical' explanation of the dualism which is more precise than what Kelsen brought

---

[25] This summary is mainly taken from Heidemann 1999: 348.

forward in *Hauptprobleme*: It is impossible that an Ought-judgment contradicts
an Is-judgment (Kelsen 1928a: 62).[26]

The most prominent version of the Is–Ought dichotomy is Kelsen's juxta-
position of causality and imputation. However, he also equates the dualism with
the seemingly ontological divide between nature and mind, nature and society,
reality and ideology. And in the manner of the neo-Kantians, he instrumenta-
lizes the Ought to thwart any psychologistic tendencies in legal science; furthermore, he mentions a theoretical Ought which is a purely formal concept,
standing for the autonomy of law or, what amounts to the same, the autonomy of
legal science.

3.2.4.1 Causality and Imputation

The main case of the dichotomy between Is and Ought, for legal science, is the
dualism between normative imputation and causality. This is expounded by
Kelsen in the foreword to the second edition of the *Hauptprobleme*:

> [T]he norm as a judgment of Ought is contrasted with the law of nature, and
> the *Rechtssatz,* which is qualified as a norm, is contrasted with the specific
> causal law of sociology. Therefore, my main concern is the *Rechtssatz* seen as
> an expression of the specific legal autonomy [*Rechtsgesetzlichkeit*]; and from
> this perspective the law of legal science is a system of *Rechtssätze,* a system
> of judgments, just as nature as the object of natural science is – for transcen-
> dental philosophy – a system of judgments. The difference lies simply in that
> the latter judgments express the causal relation of the system of nature
> whereas in the *Rechtssatz* the specific normativity of law manifests itself.
> Both in the judgment, which is the causal law, and in the *Rechtssatz,* a certain
> condition is connected with a certain consequence. But instead of the causal
> nexus, it is a different principle of connection which binds the consequence to
> the condition [in the *Rechtssatz*]. (Kelsen 1923: VI–VII, my translation)

This connection to causality, the analogon in the sphere of law, is the specific
legal Ought. Kelsen dubs it *"periphere Zurechnung"* (peripheral imputation)
(Kelsen 1992: 50 [Kelsen 1934: 57];[27] it must be distinguished from *"zentrale
Zurechnung"* (central imputation) which consists in linking an act to a person.
The background to this version of the dualism is Kelsen's specific brand of

---

[26] It is more precise because the terms '*ableiten*'/derive or '*(be-)gründen*'/ground (which Kelsen
uses) are not well defined. A sophisticated formulation of the dualism might run as follows: "It is
impossible to deduce a nontrivial pure normative sentence from a consistent set of sentences
which does not contain any pure or mixed normative sentences." But that does not seem to say
more, for this impossibility seems to be given exactly if Is-judgments and Ought-judgments
cannot contradict each other.

[27] As far as I can see, Kelsen never explained why he called this central normative function
"peripheral imputation" and denoted the rather unimportant ascription of an act to a person (a
person being just a reification of a set of norms) as "central imputation."

neo-Kantianism according to which the object of cognition must be an *Urteilszusammenhang*, a coherent set of valid cognitive judgments. These judgments must be hypothetical judgments, that is, judgments of the form "*if a, then b*," because the objectivity of cognition demands that it is expressed by, or can be derived from, universal propositions (what Kelsen calls "*Gesetzlichkeit*"; Kelsen 1923: VII). The category of peripheral imputation constitutes the *Rechtssatz*, the general legal norm qua cognitive hypothetical judgment, by joining together two states of affairs and determining that if one is given, the other (an exercise of coercion) ought to follow. As such, it does not have much in common with the 'classical' practical Ought; it is just a purely formal linkage. There is no norm-subject, and there is no a priori content of any legal norm, that is, some legal content which is valid without some explicit legislative or judicial act whose 'meaning' it is. In *Allgemeine Staatslehre* Kelsen gives the following 'average' formula for the general norm: "If Ha + C (or Hna + C), then Co>H," that is, if a human being acts in way a (and certain conditions are fulfilled), or if a human being fails to act in way a (and certain conditions are fulfilled), then coercion ought to be exerted (normally against this human being) (Kelsen 1925: 49).

Perhaps this relation, which is closer than material implication and not quite the same as entailment, can best be explained by the notion of a deontically perfect world: In a deontically perfect world, that is, in a world where no norm is violated, coercion follows upon fulfillment of the conditions with the necessity of a law of nature.

A notable by-product of this conception is that legal norms, being logical judgments, are as a matter of course capable of standing in logical relations – an issue that will become a major problem in Kelsen's third and fourth phases.[28]

Kelsen, like Kant, takes Ought-judgments to be objectively valid, that is, genuine cognition. But, as noted in Section 2.2, Kant has it that practical cognition, cognition of Ought, is a special function of reason, while empirical cognition is the result of an interplay of understanding with intuition, of concepts with nonobjective perceptual material delivered by the senses. By contrast, Kelsen's conception of legal cognition is an exact analogy to empirical cognition. The Ought, for him, is not a concept of reason, but a category of relation, constituting a judgment which processes empirical material, guided by the rules determined in a "higher" norm:

> I have maintained that questioning the specific validity of an individual legal rule leads – step by step – to a next higher legal rule and finally to the basic

---

[28] See Section 3.3.5 for the third phase and Section 3.4.6 for the fourth phase.

norm, while questioning the content of the legal rule, i.e. asking why a single legal rule of a specific legal system has just this and no other content, leads to the legislative acts or judicial judgments which constitute the "material" of the *Rechtssätze*. This distinction is analogous to the distinction between concept and perception, between the logical form and its perceptual material, made in transcendental philosophy. I have distinguished between the "content", meaning the material still to be formed, and "validity", meaning the form of the material when construed into a valid logical judgment. ... The logical creation of the law ... from the basic norm proceeds step by step and under constant reference to a parallel fact. (Kelsen 1922a: 214–5, my translation)

This is one of Kelsen's first depictions of the legal hierarchy, the *Stufenbau* of law. It is noteworthy that the higher legal norms do not employ the category of imputation; rather, they are meta-rules stating empirical criteria for lower norms to be valid. I will come back to this point later (Section 3.2.5). For now, it suffices to say that peripheral imputation, for Kelsen, is identical with the legal Ought; it is a purely formal category of relation employed in the hypothetical judgments of legal science whose content and validity depend on factual acts which are named as criteria for the norm's validity in "higher" rules.

3.2.4.2 Nature and Mind, Reality and Ideology, Nature and Society

Kelsen's most prominent and coherent interpretation of the dualism of Is and Ought in his neo-Kantian phase has it that these elements are identical with causality, in the sphere of nature, and (peripheral) imputation, in the sphere of law. However, Kelsen brings forward several other explanations of the dualism.

One strand of explanation is seemingly an ontological one. Kelsen declares the dualism of Is and Ought to be identical with, constitutive of, or derivative from, the dualisms of nature and mind, reality and ideology, nature and society. It is not necessary to go into detail regarding these ontological versions of the dualism, because they do not concern the legal Ought as part of the transcendental-idealistic approach. Kelsen himself summarizes them in one grand sweep as follows:

The conditions, stemming from the sphere of causally ordered events, for the genesis of certain representations (understood as psychic acts) of norms might be called the "real substructure" on which the norms and systems of norms, as specific ideal contents, rise like a superstructure, as "ideologies" which are *autonomous* vis-à-vis the natural laws governing the substructure. But this is just an image, borrowed from the terminology of the materialist conception of history, for the relation between the systems of *nature* and *mind*, and, hence, between the systems of "reality" and of value, of which the relation between nature and society is a special case. (Kelsen 1925: 21, my translation)

There is one important manifestation of this dualism which will later be discussed in a bit more depth (Section 3.3.5): the dualism between a psychic intentional act and its ideal meaning-content, as introduced by Husserl when fighting against psychologism. The psychic act is part of nature. The Ought is an ideal or abstract content, so it belongs to the level of the meaning of the act. On the one hand, Kelsen emphasizes that both levels are autonomous; on the other, he maintains that it is peculiar for meaning-contents always to be sustained by psychic acts (Kelsen 1920: 97 fn.; Kelsen 1922b: 81 fn.).

3.2.4.3 Ought and Validity

In the second phase, the notion of validity is, superficially, defined as it was in the first phase; it is the "specific existence" (Kelsen 1992: 12 [Kelsen 1934: 7]) of the norm which consists in the fact that one should 'really' behave in the way determined by the norm. This definition of validity stays constant throughout all phases of the Pure Theory.[29] Kelsen rarely explains it in detail; but in the neo-Kantian context, validity is not special to normative judgments; rather, it is the 'logical' existence of any cognitive judgment which is given if the sentence expressing the judgment is true. It is normatively charged itself. Among the most challenging parts of all Kelsen's writings are those passages in *Staatsbegriff* and *Rechtswissenschaft und Recht* where he deals with Husserl, Windelband, the concept of validity, normative logic, and psychologism. They mark two of the few occasions where he delved somewhat deeper into neo-Kantian philosophy, and they are remarkable for the philosophical flights he was sometimes ready to take. In *Staatsbegriff* Kelsen writes:

> Even in my *Hauptprobleme*, in order to explain the non-psychological meaning of the Ought, which, if attributed to any content, is completely different from the assertion that anybody wants or wishes this content, I referred to the depiction which Husserl gave of this problem in his *Logische Untersuchungen*, 2nd ed., 40 ff. In this connection, I want to call attention

---

[29] In secondary literature, Kelsen's concept of validity is widely held to be obscure, covering different things, like the existence of the norm, its binding force, its being a member of the legal system, etc. (see, e.g. Nino 1998 and the papers by E. Bulygin and E. G. Valdés in the same volume). This is not justified; the core of Kelsen's conception of validity is clear throughout all the phases: The norm, that one ought to do *a*, is valid (i.e. in the neo-Kantian context, is a valid ought-judgment) exactly if one 'really' ought to do *a*, or, which means the same, if the sentence "one ought to do *a*" is true. In a similar way, the question whether the legal *Ought* is a "legitimate" or "justified" Ought is idle (on this question, see, e.g. Paulson 2012). The legal norm is "binding," "legitimate," or "justified," exactly if it is valid, that is – again – if one 'really' ought to do what the norm says. But this validity is relative to the frame of reference of the established practice of legal dogmatics; as a matter of course, a legal norm can only decree what ought to be done legally. Inside the autonomous 'language game' of law, one 'really' ought to do what the law says. But there might still be reasons for not letting this language game determine how one acts.

to the far-reaching parallel between the dualism of the ideal normative-juridic view and the real causal-psychological view and the dualism, depicted brilliantly by Husserl, between the ideal-normative-logical and the real-psychological view (cf. especially Husserl, ibid., 50 ff.). It cannot be investigated in this place how far the parallel reaches. But it is remarkable that normative logic, which stands in contrast to psychological logic, tends to become pure logic, just as the normative theory of law and state, which stands in contrast to sociological theory, tends to become a pure theory of law and state. I cannot determine whether the "pure" logic can no longer be a "normative" logic, as Husserl maintains. But it strikes me that Husserl's terminology is not quite clear in this regard. Although he replaces the dualism of Is and Ought, natural law and norm, by the dualism between natural law and ideal law, real science and ideal science, although he abominates the identification of ideality and normality and wants to conceive the "pure" logic as a system of theoretical sentences, not as a system of norms, he himself talks about the fundamental difference between the purely logical norms and the "technical rules of a specific human craft" of thinking. . . . And it seems not to be a coincidence that especially those theorists who oppose the psychologist logicians by setting up logic as a normative discipline (Kant, Herbart, Drobisch, Sigwart) postulate a "pure" logic at the same time. For them, the "Ought" achieves "purity" vis-à-vis psychology, just as it does for the theory of law and state vis-à-vis psychological sociology as a natural science. (Kelsen 1922b: 81 fn., my translation)

And in *Rechtswissenschaft und Recht* he maintains:

The pivotal point for the non-psychological meaning of Ought which is independent of any human subjectivity is what Kant claimed emphatically and in all clearness: The validity of the judgment that something ought is independent from the validity of the judgment that this something is, was, will be, or even can be. This independence of Ought-validity from Is-validity, i.e., the validity of the being of nature, must by necessity exclude any reference to the actual wanting or wishing, recognising or acting of the content of the Ought on the part of the human being at whom the Ought is "directed". The Ought . . . in the judgments of legal science, i.e., the legal rule, is no more directed at a human being than the law of nature is. . . . Striving for a non-psychological meaning of the legal norm as an Ought-judgment, I am in the same situation as the logicians vis-à-vis the logical norm. In his *Prinzipien der Logik*, Windelband says about the pure logic: "*It does not teach how one really thinks, but how one ought to think if one wants to think correctly. This common definition suffices to express the principal demarcation of logic against psychology: But it must not be overlooked that the formulation makes allowance for the fundamental fact of empirical thinking, mentioned above, that it is prone to the possibility of error, . . . so that one has to take care that the validity of these forms is in the last instance completely independent from the striving of empirical and especially human consciousness for knowledge. . . . From this it follows that all laws of logic have a double status: On the one hand, they are rules for empirical consciousness, which all thinking ought to comply with, if striving for truth. On the other hand, their inner meaning and being is completely independent from the question whether there are any mental processes which are in accordance with them or not. The latter might be called their validity per se, the former, their validity for us. . . . From 'our' perspective, logic is an 'Ought'. But this Ought must ground in something whose validity exists per se and which becomes a norm, an Ought, only by being related to a consciousness capable of error."* The double meaning of the logical norm, its validity per se, that is its "objective" validity, . . . and its validity for us corresponds to the objective validity of the legal norm claimed by me, and its subjective validity which might better be called "efficacy". . . . The Ought is the suitable expression precisely for this objective validity of the logical law, the validity per se; accordingly, Windelband himself emphasizes that this Ought expresses the demarcation of logic against psychology. (Kelsen 1922a: 206–8, my translation, italics added)

These passages build a bridge to the neo-Kantian discussion concerning validity and normativity described above, and they are a key to understanding Kelsen's concepts of Ought and validity: Kelsen sides with Windelband in saying that validity is what distinguishes objective meaning-contents from natural world objects; he also holds that validity is a normative concept. He chooses to differ, however, as far as the question whether 'Ought' is an adequate expression for this normative feature of validity is concerned. In their attempt to fend off any psychologistic connotations, Husserl and Windelband answer in the negative, because the Ought refers to human subjectivity. Husserl grounds normativity in a sphere of ideality, while Windelband anchors it in the sphere of values. Both run the danger of falling prey to Platonism; this problem was discussed in the first part.[30] Not so Kelsen: For him, the Ought is an adequate expression of this kind of objective normativity; he thinks that the psychological connotations of the Ought are taken care of by distinguishing between normative validity and factual efficacy (in the special sense of the meaning-content being in sufficient degree embodied in psychic acts). He adds that there is no individual who the legal norm is directed at, anyway; after all, the hypothetical normative judgment of legal science has no addressee.

I tend to think that Kelsen is right. There is, however, a problem. Equating the Ought with normative validity results in a peculiar duplication of the Ought. On the one hand, the legal Ought is identical with the cognitive category of peripheral imputation, which is at work *inside* the hypothetical judgment of the *Rechtssatz*. On the other hand, the Ought is identical with the validity of the *Rechtssatz* as a judgment, which is a matter of its logical existence. This kind of

---

[30] See Section 2.3.3

Ought is not specific to normative judgments; it also adheres to objective Is-judgments. It might best be rendered as

> One ought to judge/think that way.

If this implicit normative element is made explicit, a valid *Rechtssatz* might be formulated, using two different kinds of Ought, as

> One ought$_1$ to judge/think that, under conditions c, coercion ought$_2$ to be exerted.

Kelsen does not clearly distinguish between these two types of Ought; and he sometimes, as in the passages cited above, seems to hold that the validity-Ought is quite enough to guarantee the autonomy of legal science.[31] This is distantly echoed in some less characteristic passages where Kelsen maintains that the Ought is just a formal marker, the ladder to get into the legal system; once you are inside, it makes no sense to speak of Ought and of the dualism of Is and Ought.[32] That, in turn, is vaguely reminiscent of the neo-Kantian notion that law as a social and cognitive practice is 'given,' that is, 'always there,' and that the legal Ought is problematic only 'from the outside,' or from the level of meta-theory.

3.2.4.4 The Objectivity of Ought

Kelsen holds that the Ought is a category constituting theoretical judgments of legal science; it is in a strong sense objective: If there is a norm according to which you ought to act in a certain way, then it is not just the case that someone thinks that you ought to act in a certain way; rather, you *really* ought to act in a certain way. Thus, validity and objectivity of the norm coincide.

This seems, at first sight, to be at odds with Kelsen's assumption that there can be no objective morality, that is, no objective 'absolute' Ought. For he is quite adamant on this point. In *Reine Rechtslehre*, he holds that, from the perspective of rational cognition, justice as part of social morality is just a compromise between conflicting interests. This compromise is a matter of will, not of reason (Kelsen 1992: 16–18 [Kelsen 1934: 15–16]). There is no practical reason, and there can be no absolute morality.

---

[31] When dealing with Max Weber in *Staatsbegriff*, however, Kelsen seems to argue (not quite convincingly) the other way round: Validity is not Ought$_1$, rather, Ought$_2$ is validity, so that the normative meaning of an ideology seems to guarantee its validity; see Kelsen 1922b: 162.

[32] Cf. Kelsen 1920: 10 fn. (It is a peculiarity of *Problem der Souveränität* that the footnotes are often more significant than the main text. Kelsen had the text more or less finished in 1916, but publication was delayed until 1920, and some of the notes seem to have been added in the meantime. So the book mirrors Kelsen's 'thought in progress.')

However, these views might go together, even if Kelsen's relativistic view of morality is a somewhat superfluous add-on to his theory. After all, although he claims to offer a transcendental philosophy of law, this transcendental philosophy is just a critical reconstruction of legal science, which he equates with legal dogmatics, from the inner perspective. If transcendental philosophy in a neo-Kantian vein adheres to some *factum* of science, working out its essentials and presuppositions, then its perspective is at the same time internal (taking the scientific judgments to be valid) and detached (not determining whether they really are valid). It does not say that the sentences of sciences are true because their presuppositions are true (or vice versa); rather, it maintains that the presuppositions are a necessary condition for the judgments of legal dogmatics to be valid, while the validity of these judgments is a sufficient condition for the presuppositions to hold. There is a kind of relativity ingrained in taking the *factum* of legal science as a starting point. The neo-Kantian philosopher is a meta-theorist. He does not maintain:

> *As* the judgments of legal science are valid, their presuppositions hold,

or vice versa; rather he tells us:

> The judgments of legal science are the best we can get, if we want to find out what the law is, and *if* the judgments of legal science are valid, certain presuppositions hold.

3.2.5 Relations between Norms: the Legal Hierarchy and the Basic Norm

Besides founding his theory explicitly on a neo-Kantian basis, Kelsen introduces further innovations during this second phase which are related to each other: He presents the *Stufenbautheorie,* i. e. the theory of a hierarchy of legal norms, and the concept of a 'basic', or rather 'apex,'[33] norm.

Both conceptions are part of a solution to the 'taboo' concerning the question of the validity of legal norms. To recap: In the first phase, Kelsen's opinion was that the law consists of just one level of general norms, the *Rechtssätze*, expressing a conditioned will of the state to act in a certain way. It was regarded as a presupposition of legal knowledge that these general norms are valid. Now, Kelsen distinguishes several layers of norms. A judicial sentence or an executive order is a legal norm, as well – namely, an individual norm which is valid if it was issued in accordance with a general norm. The

---

[33] Kelsen calls it "*Grundnorm*" but actually, in the hierarchy of meta-levels, it is the highest norm of the legal system – if it belongs to the legal system at all.

general norms, in turn, are valid if they are issued in accordance with the constitution. The validity of a given constitution may be derived from its being issued in accordance with an earlier constitution; but once the justifying process arrives at the historically first constitution, it will be impossible to find a higher 'positive' norm which might invest it with validity. In this case, Kelsen says, any jurist presupposes a norm which is the ground for the validity of the highest positive legal norm. This nonpositive presupposed norm is called "*Grundnorm*," that is, basic norm.

Neither conception originated with Kelsen alone. Even though there were indications of it in Kelsen's earlier work, the conception of a basic norm was mainly developed by Alfred Verdross and Leonid Pitamic, while the *Stufenbautheorie* was developed by Adolf J. Merkl – as Kelsen himself acknowledges (Kelsen 1998a: 13 [Kelsen 1923: XV]). Ironically, both theorems are, on the one hand, often regarded as major achievements of *Kelsen's* theory, and on the other, they do not work flawlessly – they are not part of the Pure Theory 'at its best.' They are not, however, necessary ingredients of Kelsen's normativism; so I will confine myself to a few remarks.

Both conceptions are expressive of *Begründungsdenken*, or the principle of sufficient reason. Even in the first phase, Kelsen maintained that there are in principle endless chains of deriving an Is, via causal laws, from another Is, and of deriving an Ought from another Ought. But he did not elaborate this, and he did not explain how an Ought might be derived from another Ought. This explanation seems, for the legal sphere, to be achieved by the theory of the *Stufenbau*. But is it?

One problem in adequately understanding the *Stufenbautheorie* is that Merkl, its creator, tended to explain it metaphorically, by using images like that of the "cataracts" of a river, where the water is more and more refined and distributed, just as the legal Ought is when it reaches the lower levels of norms (Merkl 1917: col. 175). Kelsen is more matter-of-fact, but nevertheless the relation between a norm of a higher level and a norm of a lower level is not quite clear from his writings. There are two different versions which are not necessarily exclusive, but difficult to bring together.

According to the first, a higher norm (necessarily) regulates the "creation" and (possibly) the content of the lower norm (Kelsen 1992: 63 [Kelsen 1934: 74–5]). Now, what does this mean? In this phase Kelsen takes the legal norm to be a logical Ought-judgment; and you obviously cannot create a logical judgment in the same way you might, for example, create a painting or a cake. Still, "creating" a valid Ought-judgment can be achieved by fulfilling the conditions for the judgment to be valid, or, what amounts to the same, for the corresponding normative sentence to be true. After all, in a Fregean or neo-Kantian spirit, a true judgment in a logical sense is the same as a fact,[34] and there is nothing against saying that one can bring about (normative) facts. In this case, the higher norm is a meta-level rule. Simplified, it has a form somewhat like:

> If there is a performative/utterance under certain conditions and with a certain content, the meaning of the performative/utterance gives rise to a valid norm.

In other words, it contributes to the conditions for imputing an act of coercion to some state of affairs. The circumstances of the performative and the limitation to its content would be criteria for the (lower) norm to be valid. There would be a legal hierarchy as a logical *Stufenbau* of object- and meta-levels. There are, however, two problems. First, the higher norm as a validity-rule would not be comparable to a norm in the traditional sense (to be sure, neither is the *Rechtssatz*). Second, as a validity-rule, it does not fit into the form of the hypothetical judgment connecting a coercive act with certain conditions in a normative way. The definition of the legal norm as a hypothetical judgment is tailored to the one-level conception of law presented in the *Hauptprobleme*; it seems oddly misplaced when confronted with the *Stufenbautheorie*.

According to the second version, the higher norm serves as a scheme for transferring the Ought onto some empirical or 'alogical' material, thus bringing a new norm into existence. This version is prominent in the specific neo-Kantian writings. As a system of cognitive normative judgments, law is created by legal science, using 'higher' norms to bestow the mode of Ought or validity on some content 'given' by the empirical acts of legislature or judiciary:

> I have distinguished between content, meaning the material still to be formed, and validity, meaning the form of the material when construed into a valid logical judgment. The logical creation of the law (meaning, of course, the law of legal science, the *Rechtssätze)* from the basic norm proceeds step by step and under constant reference to a parallel fact. (Kelsen 1922a: 214–15, my translation)

And Kelsen even employs the specific Kantian terminology of the norm as a "*Schema*" for interpreting empirical material given to legal science (although he seems to have borrowed the term from Max Weber) (Kelsen 1992: 10 [Kelsen 1934: 5]).

A problem with this version is that Kelsen sometimes comes close to saying that the empirical law-giving act, as a performative, is somehow transformed into a norm by applying the higher norm as an interpretive scheme (Kelsen 1925: 249). This is not, of course, the case; the performative is just 'triggering'

---

[34] Cf. Frege 1986: 33: "Was ist eine Tatsache? Eine Tatsache ist ein Gedanke, der wahr ist" (What is a fact? A fact is a thought which is true.)

the norm. The fact which is interpreted as giving rise to law is part of evaluated reality; it is a 'legal act,' but not a norm.

But no matter which version we prefer, is the *Stufenbau* of law really a matter of deriving one norm from another, a question of a 'chain' of validity or Ought? In the case of Is, or causality, it is indeed possible to construct a chain by stating that a causes b, b causes c, c causes d, and so on. But there seems to be no equivalent for such a chain in the legal sphere.[35] The lower norm is not determined or 'grounded' by the higher norm alone. Without the performative of the law-giving act, there would be no 'derived' norm. Accordingly, the Is-sphere and the Ought-sphere seem to mingle. Kelsen tries to get out of this predicament by saying that all empirical factors can just be the *conditio sine qua non* for the norm's validity, while the higher norm is the *conditio per quam* (Kelsen 1920: VI); but this is not really convincing. If the higher norm were a sufficient condition for the lower norm's validity (that is, existence), then it would be possible to deduce the lower norm from the higher norm. It is more plausible when Kelsen maintains, as in the passage cited above, that the lower norm gets its content from empirical acts, while it gets its validity from a higher norm. But this is metaphorical and vague, and in the end it comes down to the meta-level conception of the legal hierarchy: The higher norm is a meta-rule according to which, under certain conditions, the content of certain utterances or performatives is, or contributes to, a valid norm. It is a 'bridging principle,' sewing together Is and Ought.

Another major innovation in this phase is the introduction of the basic norm. There is abundant literature concerning this specific concept,[36] but as it is not really important in the present context it is not necessary to dwell on it extensively. The basic norm appears in two different characters. On the one hand, in the legal hierarchy, it is the highest norm. It answers the question why the constitution (or, rather, the historically first constitution from which its validity can be derived) is valid. One answer to this question would be to say that its validity is simply presupposed by legal science. For legal science as an existing sociocultural practice, the law is 'always there'; and as no jurist questions the validity of the constitution, its validity is presupposed. It simply is the fundamental constitutive rule for law. This, however, is not the way Kelsen proceeds. He does not hold that the validity of the constitution is presupposed (though sometimes he comes close to doing so) (cf. Kelsen 1928b: 24); rather he says that legal cognition, once justifying the validity of

---

[35] In fact, Kelsen holds the endless causal chain to be the analogue of the chain of *central imputation* (imputing an act to a person, see Section 3.2.7); central imputation, however, always ends somewhere (Kelsen 1968a: 134–5).

[36] For two prominent examples, see Paulson 2000 and Raz 1974.

a norm comes to an end for the lack of another higher positive criterion for valid norms, presupposes a norm according to which the content of a performative – be it custom or the intentional act of someone or a group exerting factual power – counts as the highest legal norm, that is, as constitution (Kelsen 1992: 56–7 [Kelsen 1934: 65–6]). But why should this be necessary? Famously, H. L. A. Hart held the basic norm to be a needless reduplication (Hart 1961: 246). If the neo-Kantian task of the Pure Theory is to reconstruct the intellectual content of a given sociocultural practice claiming normativity and objectivity, why not just say that inside this practice the constitution (or, what amounts to the same thing, its validity) is regarded as an axiom, that is, as an assumed nonverifiable judgment naming the highest criteria for validity inside the system?

For Kelsen, there are several possible reasons why this might not be sufficient. First, law, according to Kelsen, is only *positive* law; that is, any legal norm must get its content from a factual act which is in accordance with a 'higher' norm. So, for the constitution to be positive law, it must 'rest' on a performative, which fulfills the conditions for being norm-triggering, named in a yet higher norm; this higher norm cannot be a positive norm, it can only be presupposed as a basic norm. Second, the practice legal cognition is embedded in only takes the constitution to be valid if it adheres to a legal system which is effective and regularly applied in a way that takes the constitution to contain the highest criteria of legal validity. So the basic norm is necessary to capture the legal system's being conditioned by its efficacy – sometimes Kelsen even seems to identify it with the principle of efficacy.[37] Third, the 'positive' constitution often consists of disparate provisions, posited both by those who had the power to do so and by custom. To unify these provisions and, thus, the law, it is necessary to presuppose a norm under whose antecedent they can be subsumed as highest criteria for legal validity. This, in turn, is necessary so that law is a system and possible object of science.

On the other hand, and this is mainly responsible for the vast literature concerning the basic norm, Kelsen holds that it is the (or a) "transcendental-logical condition" (*transzendental-logische Bedingung*) for legal cognition, and thus for law; or a "hypothesis" in the sense of Cohen and Plato, that is, a fundamental constitutive element (*Grundlegung*) posited by cognition (Kelsen 1998b: 174). This is argued for by Kelsen in the following well-known passage:

> In formulating the basic norm, the Pure Theory of Law ... aims simply to raise to the level of consciousness what all jurists are doing (for the most part unwittingly) when, in conceptualizing their object of enquiry, they reject

---

[37] See Section 3.2.6.

natural law as the basis of the validity of positive law, but nevertheless understand the positive law as a valid system, that is, as norm, and not merely as factual contingencies of motivation. With the doctrine of the basic norm, the Pure Theory analyses the actual process of the long-standing method of cognizing positive law, in an attempt simply to reveal the transcendental logical conditions of that method. (Kelsen 1992: 58 [Kelsen 1934: 67–8])

Is this rather high-flown claim justified? In part, it is, and in part, it is not. For Kantian philosophy, transcendental-logical conditions are those conditions of cognition which make reference to objects possible. They are the categories of understanding which might be found, according to Kant, by taking the table of judgments as a guideline; so, for Kelsen, who levels out the difference between cognitive judgment and cognitional object and only takes into account hypothetical judgments, they are identical with the 'connector' inside these judgments. Peripheral imputation, the specific legal Ought constituting the hypothetical judgment of the *Rechtssatz*, is such a category of relation. It might truly be said to be a transcendental-logical condition. The basic norm, on the other hand, is not identical with the category of Ought; rather, it is a presupposed, most fundamental rule offering criteria for legal validity. And if one takes a closer look, it is not really an applicable criteria-rule, but just a necessary go-along if one takes the constitution to be valid. There is no real equivalent for this function in Kantian philosophy, and to call the basic norm a transcendental-logical condition is at least oblique. Yet, as shown, neo-Kantianism tends to downgrade transcendental philosophy to a critical meta-theory of scientific practice, that is, a critical analysis of the presuppositions of the established sciences – those implicit nonfactual conditions which are necessary to make it possible. Nothing speaks against taking the basic norm to be a transcendental-logical condition in this very weak sense of not being an object, but a general presupposition of legal science as it is practiced. These matters, however, need not be further pursued; they are not a special problem of the Is–Ought dualism or of normativism.

3.2.6 Relations between Is and Ought

Even though it is not possible, according to Kelsen, to derive an Ought from an Is, or vice versa, there are numerous relations between Is-elements and Ought-elements.

(1) Norms, as objective cognitive judgments, are abstract meaning-contents. In order to 'exist' in reality, abstract meaning-contents need a psychical act, like willing, thinking, or feeling, as their bearer. They are not 'given' without being willed, thought of, or felt, although they cannot be reduced to these psychical processes. Their validity is independent from any Is:

> The psychological determination is irrelevant for the logical validity of a notion, the truth of its content: The process of thinking which has Pythagoras' theorem as its content is irrelevant for the correctness of this theorem. (Kelsen 1920: 16, my translation)

Is-elements are the *conditio sine qua non* of Ought-elements, but not their *conditio per quam* (Kelsen 1920: 97 fn.; Kelsen 1925: 14). The empirical acts which 'bear' the abstract meaning-contents are "parallel phenomena" in a different dimension which necessarily conditions them (Kelsen 1920: 16). Talk of necessary and sufficient conditions, in this context, is again a bit awkward; the problem of "parallel phenomena" in different dimensions can be more aptly captured by the notion of 'supervenience': An element a supervenes upon an element b, if there cannot be a difference in a without a difference in b.[38] Applied to law, and put somewhat sloppily: There cannot be a change in the legal sphere without a change in empirical reality.[39] More importantly, Kelsen would probably have done better to distinguish, in this context, not only *two*, but *three* different phenomena: the abstract content as such, the empirical (neurological or psychical) act as such, and the immanent content of the psychical act – in the way Rickert did, and in spite of the (solvable) problems Rickert had. No doubt, the immanent content is always accompanied by the act itself; and we cannot imagine any difference in it while the psychic act, or its neurological counterpart, remains the same. But does Pythagoras' theorem really 'disappear' when it is not thought of, and can we not imagine that it is accompanied by very different psychical or neurological processes?

(2) A legal norm comes into existence, that is, gains validity, only as the result of empirical norm-positing acts. Either there must be a custom, a habitual application of a norm, or an intentional act of positing a norm, authorized by a higher norm, so that this norm can be regarded as valid.

(3) The validity of legal norms is conditioned by the fact that the legal system as a whole is effective (or, rather, not ineffective); either the majority of norms should be complied with in general, or the norms should be applied by the bodies responsible to exert coercion.[40] Kelsen's argument why this should be

---

[38] See, for example, Bennett and McLaughlin 2018.

[39] Recently, Monika Zalewska applied supervenience theory specifically to Pure Theory conceptions. In Zalewska 2020a: 87–8, she interprets the relation between the basic norm and the efficacy of the fundamental rules of the legal system as one of supervenience; in Zalewska 2020b, she interprets peripheral imputation (208–10) and the connection between act of will and legal norm (211) as relations of supervenience. She couples these interpretations with an ambitious attempt to gain material results from them, like the principle of equality.

[40] It is not easy to explain how a 'higher norm' validating a lower norm might be efficacious; possibly, the best solution is to say that it is efficacious if it is used by the individuals empowered by the legal system to posit norms and to execute sanctions as an interpretive scheme for validating norms.

the case is, however, rather diffuse. In *Problem der Souveränität*, he maintains that the principle of efficacy follows from an extralegal principle, namely, the principle of economy of thought (Kelsen 1920: 98–9). This principle demands that using a legal system to interpret human actions must find that most actions are in accordance with it; otherwise, it could not function as an interpretive scheme. The problem with this argument is that it cannot explain why law, which Kelsen takes to be an autonomous normative structure, must be used as an interpretive scheme in this way at all. In the first edition of *Reine Rechtslehre* he circumvents this problem in a peculiar way by pointing to the fact that the principle of efficacy is part of international law; so, as a positive norm of international law, it is at the same time the basic norm of any municipal order (Kelsen 1992: 61 [Kelsen 1934: 70–2]). And sometimes Kelsen insinuates, quite correctly, that the efficacy condition is due to legal dogmatics choosing to deal only with those legal orders that are effective (Kelsen 1920: 94).

(4) As mentioned, it is possible to use the normative ideology of law as a scheme for interpreting human acts, individuals, objects, or occurrences, that is, to give them some special meaning by relating them to norms: They might be legal acts in a narrow sense, acts of applying or positing norms; they might be criminal acts; an individual might be a judge; an occurrence might be a theft or a violation of duty. Kelsen expounds this function of legal norms in a prominent and lengthy passage at the beginning of *Reine Rechtslehre* (Kelsen 1992: 8–11 [Kelsen 1934: 2–6]), giving the misleading impression that law is interpreted reality, or that law's primary function is it to interpret reality. This, again, is not the case; law, for Kelsen, in this phase, is an autonomous system of normative judgments which might derivatively be used to characterize certain acts and objects as 'legal act,' 'theft,' 'last will,' etc.

(5) Is-judgments and Ought-judgments share an "indifferent substrate," something which is neither part of Is-reality nor of the normative sphere, but which is, in the case of Ought-judgments, that-which-ought-to-be and, in the case of Is-judgments, that-which-is (Kelsen 1968b: 38, 65; Kelsen 1922b: 99). It is some pre-objective material which is not yet determined by the categories. Kelsen does not further define it; it might be best under-stood either as a 'state of affairs'/'possible fact' or as something totally exempt from conceptualization.

(6) There are, however, two cases where, contraintuitively, Ought and Is are not related. First, the Ought does not 'aim' at an Is. The system of legal norms is self-contained and neither capable nor in need of being realised (Kelsen 1922a:

78). Second, as the *Rechtssatz* is just a hypothetical judgment connecting two states of affairs, legal norms, strictly speaking, have no addressee.

3.2.7 Normativism as Conceptual Reductionism

Kelsen no longer regards those legal concepts which are not a necessary part of law as a system of *Rechtssätze* as unproblematic constructions; rather, he takes them to be "fictions" which may grudgingly be admitted insofar as they simplify grasping the legal material. Nevertheless, one has to keep in mind that they are hypostatizations; there are not any objects that correspond to them. This is most succinctly expressed in *Problem der Souveränität*, where Kelsen criticizes contemporary legal thinking:

> [T]he view of the legal theorist, which is just as much diverted from the proper object of his cognizance – the legal norm – to other areas of cognition as it is marred by hypostatizations and fictions causing pseudo-problems, cannot get at its original object which is veiled by the desire for visualization, habitual ways of thinking and complacency of thought. Metaphors are solidified into independent entities, mere protheses of thought are posited as realities. They are like ghosts obstructing juridical cognition. (Kelsen 1920: IV, my translation)

The most prominent of these ghostly protheses of thought is the concept of state; Kelsen deems the state to be a person and the legal system and the state to be one and the same – in fact, arguing the case for this is the focus of his writings in the 1920s. In a similar way, both the natural and the legal person are identical with parts of the legal system: sets of norms regulating the behavior of one or several individuals (Kelsen 1992: 46–50 [Kelsen 1934: 52–7]). This regulation of behavior is a function of the secondary norms of 'duties' and 'rights,' which, in turn, can be reduced to the necessary barebones of law: A legal duty is just part of the impersonal objective *Rechtssatz*; not performing it is part of the conditions for triggering the imputation of coercion. The subjective right is a higher-level part of these conditions; its exercise triggers the existence of a duty (Kelsen 1992: 43–5 [Kelsen 1934: 47–52]). Both duties and rights and certain human acts can be connected to a person by "central" imputation, which must be distinguished from "peripheral" imputation; as a person is identical with a system of norms, this does not mean any more than that they are part of the content of a set of norms (Kelsen 1992: 50 [Kelsen 1934: 57]).

Ironically, the Pure Theory set out as an analysis of an existing practice that makes a claim to objectivity, taking seriously the normative talk contained in this practice:

> If one deprives the norm or the "ought" of meaning, then there will be no meaning in the assertions that something is legally allowed, something is legally prescribed, this belongs to me, that belongs to you, X has a right to do this, Y is obligated to do that, and so on. In short, all the thousands of statements in which the life of the law is manifest daily will have lost their significance. (Kelsen 1992: 33 [Kelsen 1934: 35])

And it ends up by reducing these normative elements of everyday legal life to the theoretical hypothetical judgment of the *Rechtssatz,* which, as a general law, is the only irreducible element of the legal sphere, securing its objectivity, not being directed at anybody.

The extensions of these secondary legal concepts cannot be determined by relying on the structure of the primary legal norm alone. For all elements conjointly making up the conditions for imputing coercion are logically equal, whether it be a delict, an exertion of a right, or some action of an attorney. Additionally, the content of the specific legal system has to be considered. This forces Kelsen to distinguish "*Rechtswesensbegriffe*" (concepts concerning the essence of law) from "*Rechtsinhaltsbegriffe*" (concepts concerning the content of law). While *Rechtsinhaltsbegriffe* are not necessary for defining law, they structure its content and are dependent on it. *Rechtswesensbegriffe* are necessary for defining the law (Kelsen 1925: 18); they consist of the *Rechtssatz,* its elements, and its presuppositions and consequences (Kelsen 1925: 60, 262–5).

3.3 The Third Phase: Commonsense Realism

The transition from Kelsen's second to his third phase marks a break in the philosophical development of the Pure Theory. Kelsen abandons neo-Kantian transcendental idealism and instead turns to a naive form of commonsense realism, according to which legal norms are not identical with the cognitive judgments of legal science; rather, the latter just descriptively reproduce the norms which are "given" to them (Kelsen 1957a: 268).

Kelsen scarcely makes the realist premises explicit, and he does not explain why he thought this change of paradigm necessary. There seem to be two main reasons. First, in the late 1930s, Kelsen dabbled in diverse nonlegal theoretical matters, in physics and in 'ethno-sociology' or cultural history, among other areas.[41] What he found unsettled his assumption that causality, as an a priori category, was the fundamental constituting principle of natural science. Modern physics taught him, or so he thought, that a rationally refined causal principle could only be conceived as expressing a statistic regularity. Ethno-sociology taught him that causality was no stable or fixed principle; rather, it eventually

---

[41] See especially Kelsen 1941.

emerged in diverse cultures from the normative principle of retribution. During a chaotic transition period in the 1930s, Kelsen seems to drop Kantian and neo-Kantian philosophy altogether and to prefer Hume's theory of causality, as well as Hume's version of the Is–Ought dualism (Kelsen 1939: 129). Kelsen had constructed the legal category of Ought, that is, peripheral imputation, in strict analogy with the (neo-)Kantian category of causality. Therefore, deconstructing the concept of causality shook the basis of his theory. Second, there might be a biographical reason. The rise of National Socialism and the beginning of the Second World War forced him to emigrate from Europe to the United States in 1940. While neo-Kantianism, although on the wane, was still a philosophical trend in Central Europe, it was practically nonexistent in the United States, at least as far as legal theory was concerned. Pragmatism and legal realism ruled the day. Thus, Kelsen had lost his institutionalized zone of discourse.[42]

Kelsen's writings during this phase need not be treated extensively here (even though they include what is widely regarded as Kelsen's opus magnum, the heavily reworked second edition of *Reine Rechtslehre* from 1960), for two reasons. First, he altogether avoids digging any deeper into the metaphysical foundations of his theory. Second, a main tenet of his theory survived the change of paradigm seemingly unscathed, namely, the thesis that law exclusively consists of norms so that all legal concepts must be reducible to legal norms. Therefore, in what follows I will confine myself to outlining Kelsen's new epistemology and its repercussions for his theory.

3.3.1 Normative Realism

To see what the turn in Kelsen's theory around 1940 amounts to, it is instructive to compare two short programmatic writings, one from the neo-Kantian phase and one from the realist phase: Kelsen's foreword to the second edition of *Hauptprobleme der Staatsrechtslehre* (1923), on the one hand, and *The Pure Theory of Law and Analytical Jurisprudence* (1941), on the other (both are easily accessible in English). According to its foreword, *Hauptprobleme*

> takes as its point of departure the fundamental dichotomy between *Sollen* and *Sein* [*Ought* and *Is*]. ... Following Wilhelm Windelband's and Georg Simmel's interpretation of Kant, I take the "ought" as the expression for the autonomy of law – with the law to be determined by legal science – in contradistinction to a social "is" that can be comprehended "sociologically". The *norm* qua *ought*-judgment, then, is contrasted with the law of nature, and the reconstructed legal norm (*Rechtssatz*), understood as a norm qua *ought*-judgment, is contrasted with the law of causality that is specific to sociology.

---

[42] See Paulson 1988a.

For me, therefore, the core problem becomes the *reconstructed legal norm*, understood as the expression of the specific lawfulness, the autonomy, of the law. . . . And from this point of view, the law that is the subject-matter of legal science emerges as a system of reconstructed legal norms, that is to say, as a series of judgments. In the same way, nature – the subject-matter of natural science – represents for transcendental philosophy a system of judgments. (Kelsen 1998a: 4–5)[43]

According to *The Pure Theory of Law and Analytical Jurisprudence*,

if jurisprudence is to present law as a valid system of norms, the proposi-tions by which it describes its object must be "ought" propositions, statements in which an "ought", not an "is", is expressed. But the proposi-tions of jurisprudence are not themselves norms. They establish neither duties nor rights. Norms by which individuals are obligated and empowered issue only from the law-creating authority. The jurist, as the theoretical exponent of the law, presents these norms in propositions that have a purely descriptive sense, statements which only describe the "ought" of the legal norm. It is of the greatest importance to distinguish clearly between legal norms which comprise the object of jurisprudence and the statements of jurisprudence describing that object. These state-ments may be called "rules of law" in contradistinction to the "legal norms" issued by the legal authority. (Kelsen 1957a: 268)

According to the earlier text, legal norms are constituted by, or identical with, the normative judgments of legal science. According to the later text, it is of the "greatest importance" to confine jurisprudence to "describing" the legal norms which are "given" to it.

But it is not only commonsense realism which is the more or less tacit background assumption of Kelsen's theory in this phase; he comes close to advocating *legal* realism, as well. Again, he does not do so explicitly. But it is conspicuous that he avoids any terminology which might imply that legal norms are abstract entities, belonging to a sphere of ideality. While speculating, in the neo-Kantian phase, that the spheres of ideality and of normativity might con-verge, and speaking of validity as the "ideal" existence of the norm, there is no longer any such talk. With some justification, Alf Ross wrote that it was only the undefined concept of validity which detained Kelsen from becoming a legal realist in this phase (Ross 1957: 564–70).

---

[43] There is a caveat concerning Paulson's translation: Rendering "*Rechtssatz*" as "reconstructed legal norm" conceals the fact that the *Rechtssatz*, though identical with the legal norm, is constituted as a *logical judgment* by legal science and that there is no normativity prior to the *Rechtssatz*; so it is not a matter of reconstruction, but of *constitution*. For my own translation see Section 3.2.4.

3.3.2 Overview: Consequences of the Realist Approach

The consequences of this commonsense realism for Kelsen's theory are rather devastating; they can be summarized as follows:

(1) The categories of Is and Ought can no longer be classified as "forms of cognition"; rather, they must be forms of reality. Kelsen, however, recoils from acknowledging that there might be something like a "normative reality." Accordingly, his explanation of the Is–Ought dualism dwindles down to the not further developed thesis that an Ought-sentence cannot be derived from an Is-sentence (and vice versa) (Kelsen 2005: 5–6 [Kelsen 1960: 3]).

(2) The status of the legal norm becomes hazy. Although Kelsen defines 'norm' as the meaning of an intentional act directed at human behavior (Kelsen 2005: 4–5 [Kelsen 1960: 4]), he neither explains what 'meaning' comes up to in a realist context, nor elucidates how the (objective) meaning of an intentional act can become the object of a cognitive judgment. Besides, the counterpart of the legal norm in the sphere of Is becomes doubtful. In the neo-Kantian phase, the (general) legal norm and the causal law, as hypothetical judgments, were juxtaposed. Now it seems as if the empirical fact from causally ordered reality is the equivalent of the norm in the sphere of Is, while the natural law is part of the cognitive level – its counterpart in the Ought-sphere is the *Rechtssatz*, which is now defined as the judgment of legal science *describing* the legal norm.[44]

(3) The possibility of a logic of norms gets problematic. Kelsen assumes that the rules of logic are effective between norms "indirectly," that is, mediated by the sentences describing the norms (Kelsen 2005: 205–6 [Kelsen 1960: 210]); but this solution is rather absurd. It seems to be a remnant of the neo-Kantian epistemology, but it is not compatible with holding that norms are "given" to cognition.

(4) The status of the basic norm becomes ambivalent: On the one hand, it is part of the sphere of objects, because it is a norm which is described by the major premise of a syllogism establishing the validity of the constitution;[45] on the other hand, it does not rest on an intentional act directed toward human behavior, but on an act of thinking, and it is not the object, but a presupposition of legal cognition (Kelsen 2005: 9–10, 23 [Kelsen 1960: 9, 23]). These aspects are scarcely compatible with each other; the basic norm does not make much sense in a realist context.

---

[44] This is not clear, however. See Kelsen 2005: 76 (Kelsen 1960: 80), for the natural law being placed on the cognitive level, and Kelsen 2005: 75 (Kelsen 1960: 78), for the causal principle being at work in nature.

[45] See Section 3.3.5.

(5) In addition, the role of legal science becomes questionable. On the one hand, it is restricted to describing the legal norms given to it; on the other hand, the legal norms are just the result of an interpretation by the legal scientist (Kelsen 2005: 45–7 [Kelsen 1960: 46–8]). It is difficult to see how these tenets might go together.

3.3.3 Causality, Imputation, and Empowerment

Even though Kelsen's engagement with the results of modern physics and cultural history had shattered his belief that causality and imputation were original and equal-ranking categories of cognition, he does not express his doubts in the main text of this period, *Reine Rechtslehre* (1960). And the dualism, for him, is still one of the manifestations of the more fundamental dualism of Is and Ought. But it loses importance and, without its defining neo-Kantian context, is somehow an alien element in Kelsen's theory. He has difficulty in ascribing imputation either to the sphere of objects or to the level of cognition. According to some passages, it is a connection on the level of the norms themselves (Kelsen 2005: 77–8 [Kelsen 1960: 81]); in other places, it appears to be a connection on the level of norma-tively interpreted reality (Kelsen 2005: 76 [Kelsen 1960: 79]). According to a third explanation, imputation is a principle which is applied when *describing* a normative order of human behavior (Kelsen 2005: 76 [Kelsen 1960: 79]), while causality rather connects the elements making up nature and is described by the natural laws (Kelsen 2005: 75 [Kelsen 1960: 78]). Yet this would not be coherent. If cognition is just a descriptive isomorphous reproduction of a world 'given' to it, then a description of a norm cannot employ the principle of imputation, unless this principle is given in some way in the normative world itself.

This matter, however, need not further be discussed here. For imputation, which was the most fundamental Ought-modality in the neo-Kantian phase, steps back together with the assumption that the legal norm is identical with the impersonal judgment of legal science. It is superseded by a very different normative function.

Kelsen now regards the Ought as a portmanteau concept, covering different kinds of normative functions: commanding, prohibiting, permitting, empower-ing, and derogating (Kelsen 2005: 4–5 [Kelsen 1960: 4–5]).[46] And the norma-tive function of the general legal norm – and, thus, the primary normative function in law – is "empowerment" (Kelsen 2005: 25, 56–7 [Kelsen 1960: 26, 57–8]);[47] all other normative functions are part of "dependent" norms which can be reduced to the general norm.

---

[46] Thus, other than in the second phase, the legal norm has an addressee.
[47] On this topic, see especially Paulson 1988b.

Basically, the general norm says that, under certain conditions, somebody is empowered to exert coercion. How can somebody be empowered to exert coercion? Kelsen distinguishes two ways of conceiving the general norm (Kelsen 2005: 57, 231 [Kelsen 1960: 57–8, 237]). From a "dynamic" perspective, the law is a hierarchy of norms. General norms constitute just one of several levels; they decree that under certain conditions a judge is empowered to issue an individual norm. "Empowerment" in this case means that the judge is able to bring about the conditions for the individual norm (the sentence she pronounces) to be valid; so this empowerment does not directly concern the exercise of coercion as a brute act but only the *ordering* of an act of coercion. From a "static" perspective, comparable to the conception of *Hauptprobleme*, there is just one level of law, the level of heavily inflated (because they contain all conditions for legally exercising coercion) general norms that run, in simplified form, something like:

> If the constitution validates a law which empowers a judge, under certain conditions, to decree that an act of coercion ought to be performed, and if under such conditions there is such a decree, then the act of coercion ought to be performed.

In both cases, the normative function is that of empowerment. In the case of the general norm according to the dynamic perspective, empowerment confers the ability to fulfill the conditions for an individual norm to be valid; in the case of the general norm according to the static perspective, it confers the ability to perform an act of coercion which is qualified as a 'legal act.' So empowerment is, in a way, the successor to imputation as the basic normative function of legal norms. There is a direct line from attributing an act – as a legal act – to the constructed person of the state as 'willed' by it, in the first phase of Kelsen's theory, via peripheral imputation, as the relation between condition and sanction inside the *Rechtssatz* in the second phase, to empowerment, as bestowing the capacity to bring about the conditions to make a lower norm valid or to vest an act with the property of being a legal act.

3.3.4 Prescriptive and Descriptive Ought; Subjective and Objective Ought; Validity

As a consequence of the separation of the cognitive level of judgments from the level of "given" objects, Kelsen distinguishes a "prescriptive" from a "descriptive" Ought. The prescriptive Ought is the Ought contained in the norms, while the descriptive Ought is its descriptive reflection at the level of dogmatic judgments (Kelsen 2005: 73–5 [Kelsen 1960: 75–7]). This distinction is scarcely argued for, and Kelsen does not make a similar differentiation for the sphere of Is.[48]

Another differentiation makes more sense. Kelsen distinguishes a "subjective" Ought from an "objective" Ought. This distinction is an advancement of a similar differentiation from the neo-Kantian phase: According to Kelsen's writings before 1940, the nonnormative material given to legal cognition to be formed into a norm is the content of some human act which claims to have normative impact according to its "self-interpretation." This is its "subjective" meaning. Its "objective" meaning, that is, whether it really gives rise to an Ought, is a matter of its interpretation in the light of a valid norm (Kelsen 1992: 9–10 [Kelsen 1934: 2–5]). In a similar vein, the "objective Ought," according to Kelsen in 1960, is the "valid" ought, the "real" Ought, which is given if it is not only *claimed* that something ought to be done, but if something *really* ought to be done.[49] The subjective Ought is given – this is the most plausible interpretation if one considers the genesis of this conception – if it is (only) claimed that something ought to be done. According to another interpretation, a subjective Ought is given if someone wants somebody else to behave in a certain way.[50] The subjective Ought is bound to an intentional act, whose meaning it is, while the objective Ought is valid even if it is no longer backed by an intentional act (Kelsen 2005: 7–8 [Kelsen 1960: 7]).

So, the underdetermined concept of validity indeed seems to bear the brunt in dragging Kelsen's notion of "objective normativity" through the realist phase without succumbing either to naturalism or to Platonism. This is reminiscent of Rickert's efforts to fend off psychologism without giving in to Platonic hyper-realism as depicted in Section 2.3.2 – only, Kelsen, in this phase, lacks the appropriate philosophical background theory to argue for his case.

3.3.5 The Legal Hierarchy and the Basic Norm

In this third phase, there are two major innovations concerning the legal hierarchy. On the one hand, Kelsen leaves the opaque quasi-Kantian terminology behind in

---

[48] The distinction makes sense on a linguistic level: A prescriptive Ought might, *cum grano salis*, be said to be involved in those performatives which are uttered in order to bring a norm in to existence, while the descriptive Ought would be contained in assertions of a valid norm which do not aim to 'bring it about.'

[49] Kelsen 2005: 7–8 (Kelsen 1960: 7–8). The German original contains a footnote in which Kelsen declares that he could also have chosen the expression "real Ought" to denote the objective Ought, if it had not been for the connotation of the expression "real" (*tatsächlich*) which point to the sphere of Is.

[50] This is implied by Kelsen's most famous example of a (solely) subjective Ought: the command of a criminal to hand over money; cf. Kelsen 2005: 44 (Kelsen 1960: 46).

describing the relation between higher and lower norm, and he maintains that this relation can be captured in the form of a syllogism. On the other hand, he brings forward the odd thesis, mentioned in Section 3.3.2, that logical relations are at work between the given norms not directly, but indirectly, mediated by the judgments or statements about the norms. The (statement of the) higher norm plays the role of the major premise in this syllogism, determining factual conditions for the existence or validity of the lower norm. The minor premise is the (statement of the) fact fulfilling these conditions; the conclusion is the (statement of the) lower norm. In Kelsen's own words:

> The foundation of the validity of a positive norm, that is, one established by an act of will and prescribing a certain behaviour, is the result of a syllogistic procedure. In this syllogism, the major premise is the assertion about a norm regarded as objectively valid, according to which one ought to obey the commands of a certain person, that is, one ought to behave according to the subjective meaning of these commands; the minor premise is the assertion of the fact that this person has commanded to behave in a certain way; and the conclusion is the assertion of the validity of the norm: that one ought to behave in this particular way. Thus the norm whose validity is stated in the major premise legitimizes the subjective meaning of the command, whose existence is asserted in the minor premise, as the command's objective meaning. (Kelsen 2005: 202 [Kelsen 1960: 205])

The main flaw of this passage has been mentioned: The idea of an "indirect" logic of norms is absurd; there is no way that a norm understood as a nonpropositional entity in a realist sense could be subjected to a propositional calculus. This apart, there are two possible ways of reconstructing the syllogism. According to the first, the major premise, simplified, would run as follows:

> If there is a (normative) utterance 'n' under certain conditions and with a certain content, then 'n' is true (so n is a valid norm).

This is comparable to the conception of the preceding phase: The higher norm would not be a norm in the usual sense, but a rule of a meta-level that states criteria for a lower norm to be valid, or, what amounts to the same, for a statement about a norm to be true. According to the second reconstruction, the higher norm does not just state general validity conditions; rather, it directly establishes an Ought for the addressees of the lower norms. Simplified, it runs as follows:

> If the legislator (or some other body) has, under certain conditions, commanded you to do a, then you ought to do a.

This sounds more like a genuine norm. However, either the lower norm is superfluous or the Ought is, again, reduplicated. If 'Oa' can be inferred from '(If c, then Oa), and c,' then there is no normative surplus in it. After all, a syllogism does not create 'new' truths; it just makes explicit conceptual relations. This seems to be different in the meta-level reconstruction, because the meta-level rule does not contain an Ought. Besides, only the meta-level reconstruction seems to capture the feature that the Ought-function, on all levels of the hierarchy, is empowering (not commanding).

Anyway, neither reconstruction really corresponds to what one would normally expect a derivation of an Ought from another Ought to look like, and both express the necessary role of 'higher' rules – no matter whether they are norms or meta-rules – in naming factual criteria for the existence of lower norms. Positivistic normativism is not possible without such rules.

Even though the basic norm, as the highest (or most fundamental) norm, survives Kelsen's turn to realism seemingly unscathed, it is, like imputation, an alien element in the realist phase. It is described by the major premise of the most fundamental syllogism in the legal hierarchy, establishing the validity of the constitution. It is still called a "hypothesis" (Kelsen 1957b: 260–2) and a "transcendental-logical condition," the latter with the restriction that this term is used *per analogiam* (Kelsen 2005: 201–2 [Kelsen 1960: 203–5]). But it is difficult to see what this analogy might look like. Transcendental-logical conditions are only conceivable as necessary conditions of cognition; having a system of 'given' legal norms depend on a presupposition of cognition is, however, contradictory. Either the norms are given to cognition, but then they cannot depend on a quasi-transcendental-logical condition; or they depend on a condition of thinking, but then they are not 'given' to cognition.

3.3.6 Relations between Is and Ought

Compared to the second phase, there are several changes concerning possible relations between Is and Ought.

First, the theory of the "indifferent substrate" is not dropped, but neglected. Kelsen just vaguely talks of a "something" which either might be the case, or ought to be the case, as the possible common or comparable content of Is and Ought (Kelsen 2005: 6 [Kelsen 1960: 6]).

Second, the norm, as an objective meaning-content, is conditioned by, or the meaning of, an intentional act, which belongs to the Is-sphere and is directed at somebody else's behavior (Kelsen 2005: 4–6 [Kelsen 1960: 4–6]). It is not quite clear what Kelsen means by an "intentional act." Considering his philosophical background, one might reasonably assume that the term is borrowed from Husserl's philosophy. For Husserl, an intentional act is a psychic act directed at some (propositional or nonpropositional) object. So a norm is the meaning of a psychic act directed at the propositional object "that someone acts in a certain way."[51] Sometimes, Kelsen seems to hold that such an act is an act of will. But this would contradict his former theses that one might only will one's *own* behavior, that norms are not necessarily connected with a 'real' act of will, and that possibly there is no psychic function of willing at all which is not a normative construct.[52] And Kelsen does not maintain that being the meaning of an act of will is a necessary feature of *any* norm. Apart from the possibility of deducing norms from other norms, there is the counterexample of the basic norm which is the meaning of an "act of thinking" (Kelsen 1960: 9).[53] Besides, it is not reasonable to condition the legal norm on an internal act of will; it is more plausible to condition it on the *expression* of a corresponding will. And this is exactly what Kelsen does in several passages.[54]

However this may be, the norm, as an Ought, has to be strictly distinguished from the act whose meaning it is. The statement that somebody ought to do *a*, cannot, for Kelsen, be reduced to the statement that somebody else wants this somebody to do *a* (Kelsen 2005: 5 [Kelsen 1960: 4]). And Kelsen maintains that

> it is entirely possible to describe the relation between a behaviour and the norm stipulating that this behaviour ought to be, without taking into consideration the act of command or custom by which the norm was created. This is obvious, for example, when we think ... of norms created by the custom of earlier generations, so that the men whose conduct is regulated by these norms are aware of them only as meanings. (Kelsen 2005: 22 [Kelsen 1960: 23])

This passage marks a central point where Kelsen's writings of the third phase differ from those of the fourth phase: He considers it possible to think of a norm without thinking of the act of will by which it came into existence.

Third, the validity of every *single* legal norm is conditioned on its efficacy (Kelsen 2005: 11 [Kelsen 1960: 11]). By contrast, in the neo-Kantian phase Kelsen conditioned (only) the validity of the whole legal system on its efficacy in general. This innovation is highly problematic. It is not argued for, and it is not quite clear how it was motivated. It does not seem to apply to statutory law; and it seems strange to say that, for example, an adjudication is invalid because

---

[51] It must be noted, though, that this interpretation is at odds with Kelsen's position, in this phase, of avoiding tagging the norm as an abstract entity.

[52] On Kelsen's changing opinions concerning the concept of will, see Section 3.4.4.

[53] Kelsen changed the relevant passage for the English translation which was published during the previous phase; in Kelsen 2005: 9–10, he maintains that it is impossible to think of a norm without thinking, along with it, of the act of will whose meaning it is.

[54] Cf. Kelsen 2005: 5 (Kelsen 1960: 4): "If an individual by his acts **expresses** a will directed at a certain behaviour of another, that is to say if he commands, permits or authorizes such behaviour – then the meaning of his acts cannot be described by the statement that the other individual *will* (future tense) behave in that way, but only that he *ought* to behave in that way" (my emphasis).

it was not subsequently carried out. This problem seems to be related to the problem of how Kelsen can account for customary law in his theory; however, it need not be pursued in this context.

Fourth, as shown, other than in the second phase, the (primary, independent) legal norm has an addressee, namely, the empowered individual.

3.3.7 Legal Concepts

As far as the reducibility of central legal concepts to the autonomous system of legal norms is concerned, there are no relevant changes. Central imputation (*zentrale Zurechnung*) is now called "attribution" (*Zuschreibung*), but it is still the relation of an act to a "person," that is, to a set of norms regulating (via secondary norms like commands or prohibitions) the behavior of one or several human beings which are identified by general criteria (Kelsen 2005: 150 [Kelsen 1960: 154–5]). The concepts of duty and (subjective) right, and the secondary norms of prescription, prohibition, etc. are 'reduced' to law as a set of (primary) norms in the same way as before (see Kelsen 2005: chapters 28–33 [Kelsen 1960: chapters 28–33]).

3.4 The Fourth Phase: The Will Theory of Norms

The fourth and last phase of Kelsen's theory comprises his writings after 1960. Around the time of the publication of the second edition of *Reine Rechtslehre*, Kelsen was engaged in an exchange by letter with Ulrich Klug who had recently published a book on the logic of law relying on modern formal logic (Kelsen and Klug 1981). Apparently influenced by Klug, Kelsen abandoned the thesis that it might be possible that logical rules define the relations not only between judgments about norms, but also, mediated by these judgments, between the norms themselves (Kelsen and Klug 1981: 48–9). Independently from the exchange with Klug, he also abandoned the thesis that a norm might be the meaning-content of an act of thinking, and tied the norm strictly to an act of will: "no norm without an act of will whose meaning it is" (Kelsen 1991: 234 [Kelsen 1979: 187]).

But there are more changes. Kelsen seems to have realized around 1960 that his philosophical background might need to be updated and expanded, and he gathered material from innumerable contemporary sources – especially from linguistic philosophy, moral philosophy, and logics – to undergird his conceptions.[55] But his theory remains something of a patchwork. This is, in part, due to the fact that there is no comprehensive monograph dealing with it as a whole. An exception seems to be *Allgemeine Theorie der Normen* (*General*

---

[55] On the literature studied by Kelsen, see Opałek 1980: 11–18.

Theory of Norms). But it was published posthumously, compiled from Kelsen's *Nachlass*. It contains many inconsistencies, and it is an open question whether Kelsen himself would have published it without major emendations.

In secondary literature, the writings of this last phase are often regarded as inducing a 'break' in the genesis of the Pure Theory, and the innovations they included are mostly rejected. The new conceptions have been berated as "norm-irrationalism" (Weinberger 1981: 94), and as destructive of the main tenets of the classical Pure Theory (Paulson 2013). But I tend to think that the 'break' in the theory occurred around 1940, and that Kelsen's writings after 1960 are an attempt to deal with the problems caused by his previous half-hearted realist conception of normativity. And if he wrecked his theory, at least he did so in style, and not by philosophical parsimony.

3.4.1 Foundations

The times of philosophical austerity are past; the foundations of the Pure Theory are fleshed out, once more, albeit in different directions. First, Kelsen sticks to the commonsensical realism from the third phase – again, without elaborating it: "As a science, legal science can only know and describe the norms which are *given* to it" (Kelsen 1991: 153 [Kelsen 1979: 123]). But at the same time, the sphere of ideality is rehabilitated; Kelsen no longer avoids calling the validity of the norm its "ideal" existence (Kelsen 1968c: 150). Second, Kelsen undergirds his theory with a theory of speech-acts on the one hand, according to which norms are based on acts of "commanding" (Kelsen 1991: ch. 10 [Kelsen 1979: ch. 10]), and a theory of intentional acts, according to which norms are based on psychic acts of will (Kelsen 1991: ch. 9 [Kelsen 1979: ch. 9]), on the other. This is supplemented by a semantic theory, according to which norms and assertions are the meaning-contents of different types of sentences.

3.4.2 Is and Ought

This new abundance in respect of the philosophical foundations of the Pure Theory has consequences for Kelsen's conception of the dualism of Is and Ought:

(1) Sometimes Kelsen still denotes Is and Ought as "categories," but he does not explain these elements in terms of neo-Kantian philosophy. Instead, citing Henry Sidgwick, he calls them "undefinable basic concepts." And he still relies on the "logical principle" that it is not possible to deduce a statement about a norm from a statement about a fact (Kelsen 1991: 58 [Kelsen 1979: 44]).

(2) In addition, there is a rudimentary ontological explanation of the dualism, according to which the Is is the aggregate of objects or occurrences subjected to causal laws, while the Ought is the aggregate of norms, understood as ideal entities (Kelsen 1968c: 150).

(3) The main explanation is based on an amalgam of semantics, linguistic pragmatics, and a theory of intentional acts. It might charitably be reconstructed as follows: Is and Ought are different modes in different classes of sentences. The Is is the mode of assertive sentences and the Ought is the mode of normative sentences. The mode of an assertive sentence is that something is the case; the mode of a normative sentence is that something ought to be the case. Both sentences have a "content" which might be the same (or at least comparable); Kelsen labels it "modally indifferent substrate" (Kelsen 1991: 60–1 [Kelsen 1979: 46]).

Sentences of these types are embedded in different pragmatics, and there are different types of intentional acts that coordinate with them: Assertive sentences are used to let somebody else know something, while normative sentences are (foremost) used to let somebody want something (Kelsen 1963: 2). Norms, as the meaning of normative sentences, are necessarily based on acts of will; propositions, as the meanings of assertive sentences, are based on acts of thinking. The concept of a 'meaning' of a sentence is not further explained by Kelsen. Sometimes he seems to think that the meaning of a sentence is identical with its Is or Ought mode (Kelsen 1963: 2; Kelsen 1991: 26 [Kelsen 1979: 21]); it would be more plausible to say that it is made up of mode and content.

This is certainly an improvement compared to the conception offered in the preceding phase. The status of the norm as a meaning-content of a sentence is clarified; and its linguistic counterpart concerning the sphere of Is is determined in an unequivocal way. However, there are new problems.

3.4.3 Subjective and Objective Ought and Their Relation to Empowerment

Again, Kelsen distinguishes a subjective from an objective Ought. The objective Ought is still defined as before; it is the valid Ought which is mandatory for its addressee (Kelsen 1991: 27 [Kelsen 1979: 22]). But while the subjective Ought appeared, in the realist phase, to be (predominantly) a purported or claimed objective Ought, it is now the subjective Ought which is more fundamental.

The subjective Ought is the meaning of an act of commanding. An act of commanding is an act of will directed at the behavior of somebody else. As it is impossible 'directly' to want the behavior of someone else – here, Kelsen resuscitates a thesis from his first phase – the meaning of the act of will is not that somebody behaves in a certain way, but that somebody *ought* to behave in a certain way Kelsen 1991: 26, 31, 44–5 [Kelsen 1979: 21, 24, 35]). Kelsen, however, does not further explain how (impossibly) willing that somebody else *acts* in a certain way miraculously transforms into wanting that he *ought* to act in a certain way.

Two aspects are noteworthy. On the one hand, Kelsen seems to think that the internal, psychic, intentional act of willing somebody to do something is, in this context, necessarily connected with giving it expression by uttering a command (Kelsen 1991: 26 [Kelsen 1979: 21]). On the other hand, it seems to be the *meaning* of Ought that someone wants somebody else to act in a certain way. Accordingly, the objective Ought seems, for Kelsen, always to be 'grounded' on a subjective Ought;[56] it is given if there has been an act of commanding (and a subjective Ought with it), which has been empowered (Kelsen 1991: 233–4 [Kelsen 1979: 27–8]).

Even if we presume that this conception is coherent, it raises a number of questions. First, from the beginning, it was Kelsen's concern to secure the status of legal science as a true, autonomous science. This affords in Kelsen's opinion, that its subject matter is both normative and objective. In the neo-Kantian phase, this was achieved by taking norms to be cognitive normative judgments; a valid normative judgment contains an objective Ought, and a subjective Ought is contained in claims or beliefs about this objective Ought. But if, in this late phase, the meaning of Ought is fully established by there being an act of commanding, how could there possibly be some surplus quality which transforms it into an 'objective' Ought, that is, morphs it into 'one *really* ought to act like this'? And what, actually, does it mean, in the will theory of norms, to say that one 'really' ought to act in a certain way? Second, and connected with the first point, what does 'empowering' mean if it does not somehow 'legitimize' the Ought claimed by someone; and can a 'legitimate' Ought mean anything but that one 'really' ought to act in the way prescribed, so that the objective Ought would, after all, be more fundamental?

Kelsen's explanation of the concept of empowerment is rather ambiguous. On the one hand, he still thinks that it is, in law, the primary normative function (Kelsen 1991: 97 [Kelsen 1979: 77]); and he defines it as "conferring on an individual the power to posit or apply norms" (Kelsen 1991: 102 [Kelsen 1979: 82–4]). But this seems to conflict with his general definition of the Ought as the

---

[56] This follows from the thesis that every norm includes and is determined by a command; Kelsen 1991: 233–4 [Kelsen 1979: 186–7].

meaning of an act of *commanding*. And so there is another explanation according to which empowerment appears as a 'conditional command': If empowerment concerns the positing of norms, it 'implies' a command:

> [B]y empowering the legislative organ to enact statutes *binding* on the
> the subjects of the law, the constitution empowers the legislator to make
> the subjects' behaviour which does not agree with the statutes the
> condition for sanctions and thereby make the statutes he enacts binding
> on the subjects of the law. Thus the subjects are bound in the last
> analysis by the constitution itself . . . . In other words, they are com-
> manded by the constitution to comply with the statutes. (Kelsen 1991:
> 104 [Kelsen 1979: 83])

There seem to be three ways of interpreting this passage: The first interpretation is that the legal system consists of just one command, contained in the constitution (or even in the basic norm), saying that one ought to obey the legislator (or the authors of the constitution); all other norms are simply 'technical rules' stating what one has to do if one wants to obey the constitution (or the basic norm). Or, on a second interpretation, we have a curious duplication of commands; it is not only the lawgivers who command that, for example, theft ought to be punished, but also the authors of the constitution. Both reconstructions seem to be slightly strange, but they are possible, of course. In both cases, empowerment could be reduced to the function of commanding. Yet, in neither case would it make sense to distinguish between a subjective and an objective Ought. Besides, as commanding or prescribing, in law, is just the function of secondary norms, there seems to be a logical circle: The normative function of primary norms, empowering, can be reduced to the normative function of secondary norms, commanding; but secondary norms can, in turn, be reduced to primary norms. The third interpretation would be to return to the conception according to which empowerment 'validates' the Ought; but then there seems to be, again, a primacy of the objective Ought, which grates harshly with the command or will theory of Ought.

3.4.4 The Will Theory of Norms and Validity

A kindred problem is the relation between the will theory of norms and the concept of validity. As shown in Section 2.3, the concept of validity was central to the formation of normativism – and to Kelsen's theory in the neo-Kantian phase. Validity, in this last phase, is again defined as the "specific existence" of the norm; it is analogous not to the truth of an assertion but to the existence of a fact: "That a norm prescribing a certain behaviour is *not* valid means that this norm does not exist. 'A valid norm' is a redundant expression. 'An invalid norm' is a contradiction in terms. . . . Truth is a property of the statement.

Validity is not a *property* of the norm, but its *existence*" (Kelsen 1991: 171 [Kelsen 1979: 137]). And, as mentioned, Kelsen no longer avoids calling this kind of existence "ideal." It consists in that the norm should be complied with or applied – independent of its recognition by the person to whom it is addressed.[57]

All this is in accordance with most of what Kelsen said in the preceding phases, but it is scarcely compatible with his strict will theory of norms. A norm exists or is valid if one 'really' ought to act in the way it prescribes. This implies, again, that the 'objective' Ought is the genuine Ought, while the subjective Ought is just a purported or claimed Ought. In contradistinction, according to the will theory the subjective Ought is fundamental; and the objective Ought is a specially qualified subjective Ought.

This opaqueness is partly due to Kelsen not really offering a clear-cut concept of an act of will; so this topic deserves a short digression. Three questions, in particular, connected with the concept of will, are not answered clearly in any of the phases of the Pure Theory:

(1) Is the act of will an internal psychic act, or is it the external expression of someone to the effect that she wishes somebody to do something?
(2) Is the act of will necessary for the existence of the norm in the sense that the norm only exists as long as there is an act of will as its 'bearer,' or is the act of will just necessary to 'trigger' the existence of the norm, so that it is possible that the norm exists while the act of will is no longer extant?
(3) Is the act of will part of the definition of the norm, or is it just a condition of its existence?

The most plausible solution, at least for the sake of reconstructing law, is that the act of will is an external act, and that it is necessary only to 'trigger' the norm. The problem is that Kelsen, in this phase, sees a much closer connection between Ought and will. Even in the neo-Kantian phase, he had an ambiguous understanding of the concept of will. Sometimes he doubted whether there could be something like a will which is not a normative construct (Kelsen 1922b: 241–5). So the will might be reducible to normativity. In other places, he took the will to be a purely psychic category (Kelsen 1922a: 182). In that case, will and Ought would be conceptually independent from each other. Then again, he defined the Ought as an impersonal objective willing (Kelsen 1920: 9 fn.), so that the will seems to at least partly define the Ought.

---

[57] But not independent of recognition altogether, cf. Kelsen, 1991: 3, 50–1 (Kelsen 1979: 3, 39–40).

But if we take seriously Kelsen's thesis from *General Theory of Norms,* that 'Ought' *means* that someone wants somebody else to act in a certain way, the conclusion that Ought and willing are *conceptually* interwoven can hardly be avoided. If we accept that, however, it would not make much sense to talk of 'validity' and of an 'objective' Ought; and the nature of empowerment would be a mystery. Normativism, as propagated by Kelsen in the 1920s, would finally have evaporated.

3.4.5 Prescriptive and Descriptive Ought; Imputation

The differentiation between a prescriptive and a descriptive Ought is slightly modified in this last phase. Kelsen still maintains that Ought sentences can be used both to describe and to posit a norm (an "imperative," by contrast, can only be used to command or to express a norm – to prescribe something) (Kelsen 1991: 150–1 [Kelsen 1979: 120–1]). Sometimes he comes close to holding that the difference is less one of the semantics but of the pragmatics of Ought sentences[58] (which seems to be correct), and sometimes he seems to say that a descriptive Ought sentence might be better formulated as a sentence about the validity of a norm (not as "*x* ought to do *a,*" but as "the norm, that *x* ought to do *a,* is valid") (Kelsen 1991: 155 [Kelsen 1979: 125]).

Somehow, the concept of imputation has managed to make it into these strange new surroundings:

> In the linking of a condition and a sanction brought about by a general moral or legal norm and described by ethics and legal science . . . we encounter a principle which is different from the principle of causality expressed in the natural laws formulated by the natural sciences. It is different, but analogous. I have suggested calling it the Principle of *Imputation.* (Kelsen 1991: 24 [Kelsen 1979: 19])

As before, it is not quite clear whether imputation is a matter at the cognitive level, a relation inside the norm, or part of normatively interpreted reality.

3.4.6 The Legal Hierarchy and the Basic Norm

Further problems, where the status of empowerment is involved, are the relation between a "higher" and a "lower" norm in the legal hierarchy, and the status of the basic norm. On the one hand, Kelsen abandons the conception of an "indirect" logic of norms – a logic that is mediated by the logic of the assertions describing the norms; on the other hand, both his will theory of norms and the conception of the norm as a nonpropositional object given to cognition seem to

---

[58] That is how I read the chapter concerning Sigwart, see Kelsen 1991: 151–3 (Kelsen 1979: 121–3).

make it impossible that there can be logical relations between norms at all (Kelsen 1991: 211, 217 [Kelsen 1979: 166, 171]).[59]

Kelsen describes the relation between a higher and a lower norm vaguely as one of "correspondence." His explanation of the relation between a general norm and an individual norm is instructive. Imagine a general norm as follows:

> If the competent judge has ascertained that somebody committed a theft, he ought to decide that this person ought to be imprisoned for one to five years.

There are two individual norms which might be coordinated to it.
(1) After ascertaining that Jones has committed a theft, the competent judge decides

> Jones ought to be imprisoned for one year.

This is, as a judicial sentence, a classical example of an individual norm; it cannot be deduced from the general norm but needs an additional act of will on the part of the competent judge. It might be seen as the result of compliance with and appliance of the general norm by the judge.

(2) But there is another individual norm involved. If the judge has ascertained that Jones committed a theft, then it seems that she – or anyone – might at least 'logically' conclude, using *modus ponens* and the rule of substitution, that she ought to decide that Jones ought to be imprisoned, so that there is a second individual norm:

> The judge ought to decide that Jones ought to be imprisoned for one to five years.

The possibility of such a logical conclusion is, however, negated by Kelsen. He holds that this individual norm is valid only if it is the outcome of an act of will on the part of the judge which is identical with her recognizing the higher norm. This recognition, again, seems, in turn, to condition the validity of the higher norm (Kelsen 1991: 239–41 [Kelsen 1979: 191]).[60]

This conception of the relation between individual norm and general norm, or "lower" and "higher" norm, has disastrous consequences. It contradicts

---

[59] I cannot delve into the conception of the relation between norms and logic according to the *General Theory of Norms* here. In short: Norms, in principle, are neither subject to the law of noncontradiction nor to the rules of inference. But there can be logical relations between concepts contained in norms, so that it is possible to derive a less general norm from a more general norm. And hypothetical norms have a logical 'if-then-structure' (which apparently doesn't allow for the *modus ponens* to be applied; also, Kelsen is not quite clear on the point whether this structure is part of the norm's content or whether [the validity of] the norm itself is conditioned). See Kelsen 1991: 249–50, 266–7 [Kelsen 1979: 201, 215–16].

[60] For a depiction of this problem, see Heidemann 2000: 275–8.

what Kelsen said when explaining the concept of validity; in that context, he maintained that the norm's validity was independent of its acceptance by the individual subjected to it. Besides, it is scarcely compatible either with normativism or with the way jurists talk about law and ascertain its validity; it is ultimately expressive of a recognition theory of law.[61]

Finally, the basic norm is probably what first comes to the mind of most legal theorists when asked what radical change occurred in Kelsen's theory after 1960. For Kelsen abandons the idea that the basic norm might be a hypothesis, resting on an act of thought, and instead maintains that it is a fiction in the sense of Hans Vaihinger's philosophy of "As if,"[62] a pragmatic mental tool to enable the grasp of phenomena that cannot be understood by employing the given conceptual apparatus. Judgments presupposing the existence of a fictive object are false, but they can be justified by their pragmatic function. A "full fiction," according to Vaihinger, contradicts reality and, besides, it is self-contradictory. Kelsen holds that the basic norm contradicts reality because there is no such thing; his new will theory of norms affords that any norm is based on a *real* act of will, and there is nothing like that to support the basic norm. It is also self-contradictory because it authorizes a highest legal authority while, as a norm, presupposing a higher authority on whose (empowered) act of will it rests (Kelsen 1991: 256 [Kelsen 1979: 206–7]).

In this context, it is not necessary to deal with Vaihinger's highly idiosyncratic philosophy. A few remarks must suffice. First, the change is less serious than it might appear at first sight. In Kelsen's third phase, the basic norm somehow oscillated between the cognitive level and the object level; now it is taken to be a 'feigned object,' which is a clarification. Yet even as a fiction, the basic norm is a presupposition of legal thinking; and Kelsen does not stop labelling it as a transcendental-logical condition of legal cognition (Kelsen 1968d: 1976). Regarding it as a fiction was occasioned by the need to accommodate the act of will necessarily connected with every norm. That is not an important matter; the real upheaval took place when Kelsen started seeing a necessary connection between any Ought and a factual act of will. Second, it is only the act of will the basic norm is

---

[61] To be fair, this problem is not just brought about by the strict will theory of norms. It is also a product of the combination, existent even in the third phase, of the thesis that the validity of each *single* norm is dependent on its efficacy, and the problem of how an empowerment norm might be effective.

[62] Hans Vaihinger (1852–1933) started as a neo-Kantian. He wrote *Die Philosophie des Als Ob* over several decades. The book, published in 1911 was a success; ten editions were produced (the last in 1927). Like many neo-Kantian texts, it is slightly quixotic (indeed, on the brink of dubiousness), combining pragmatism, positivism, and idealism.

supposed to rest upon which is not given in (natural) reality. So the (assumption of the) basic norm contradicts reality only if the latter incorporates this act of will in a way that it is part of the Is-and Ought-spheres at the same time.[63] Third, as norms, according to Kelsen in this phase, are not capable of logical relations, how could the basic norm be self-contradictory? At best, its content could be self-contradictory. But that would presuppose that "being legitimized by a higher authority" was part of its content – which is difficult to construct. It is more plausible to say that *asserting* the validity of a basic norm contradicts *normative* reality[64] and is self-contradictory, because it entails that there is a norm which establishes a highest authority while at the same time being legitimized by a yet higher authority. But even in this interpretation, it is doubtful whether the basic norm is a full fiction. For it just establishes the highest authority of positive law; nothing speaks against it being theoretically validated by a yet higher nonlegal authority.

3.4.7 Relations between Is and Ought

The most relevant new element in Kelsen's theory on the relations between Is and Ought has already been discussed: the tight conceptual connection between the norm and an act of will. Besides, Kelsen still maintains that the validity both of legal systems and of individual legal norms is conditioned by their efficacy (Kelsen 1991: 139–40 [Kelsen 1979: 112–13]). The theory of the "indifferent substrate," developed in the second phase and somewhat neglected in the third phase, is elaborated in the final phase. Discussing authors such as Edmund Husserl, Richard M. Hare, and Jørgen Jørgensen, Kelsen maintains that this substrate is the meaning of an act of thinking that is different from an assertion or a proposition. It is not modally formed and must not be understood as being "descriptive" or "indicative." An example of a modally indifferent substrate would be a behavior that might actually be the case (an Is-content) or which ought to be the case (an Ought-content) (Kelsen 1991: 58-61 [Kelsen 1979: 44-7]): "'Being-the-content-of-an-Ought' is the property of behaviour as modally indifferent substrate (just as it is the property of a cherry-stone to be contained in a cherry" (Kelsen 1991: 61 [Kelsen 1979: 47]).

---

[63] To be sure, if the act of will is not only a condition of the norm's existence, but part of the *concept* of a norm, then *every* norm would be a 'chimera,' a hybrid of an Ought-element and an Is-element – something that Kelsen abhorred throughout his earlier writings.

[64] This would, however, deviate from Kelsen's conception which takes reality – in this phase, and in the context of the basic norm – to be *natural* reality (Kelsen maintains that the basic norm contradicts reality because the act of will connected with it is not given in reality).

4 Summary

It is time for a short summary. Legal normativism may be defined as the view that law is exclusively a system of (normative) rules which are objective and impersonal, and which cannot be derived from any factuality. It is based on the dualism of Is and Ought. Hume might be regarded as the progenitor of general normativism because he pointed to the logical independence of (subjective) practical sentences from empirical or theoretical sentences. Kant followed suit, but he took practical sentences to be subjected to reason and, therefore, to be objective. In addition, he saw a primacy of practical reason over theoretical reason, and introduced normativity as indispensable for the operations of understanding, that is, for the cognition of objects. Lotze gave an ontological touch to this kind of theoretical Ought by holding that there are valid truths from which an Ought, or rules to think in a certain way, emanate. This interpretation was adopted by Windelband who took normativity in the form of values to be a basic philosophical element, and excluded any psychologistic explanation of cognition; at the same time, Windelband rather neglected the moral or practical Ought. Rickert systematized Windelband's approach. Ultimately, however, his theory foundered on the antagonism between immanent Ought and transcendent value.

In *Hauptprobleme der Staatsrechtslehre* (1911), Kelsen presents his theory as a methodology of legal dogmatics. He distinguishes Ought from Is and takes law to be completely a matter of Ought: Law is norm, and only those legal concepts which can be shown to be constructions on the basis of legal norms are legitimate. Kelsen identifies just one level of legal norms, the *Rechtssätze*, which are theoretical judgments expressing the constructed will of the state to act in a certain way under certain conditions. The Ought is somehow connected with the *Rechtssatz*, but Kelsen cannot yet determine in which way it is related.

In the second phase of his writings, between around 1920 and 1935, Kelsen introduces the theories of the legal hierarchy and the basic norm and explicitly places himself into the neo-Kantian tradition. He takes his theory to be a transcendental philosophy of law, that is, a theory of the necessary presuppositions and elements of legal cognition as embodied in legal dogmatics. The legal norm, the *Rechtssatz*, is the cognitive unit of legal science, a theoretical hypothetical judgment connecting an exercise of coercion with certain conditions by using the category of Ought, which Kelsen dubs "peripheral imputation." The *Rechtssatz* is the normative analogue of the causal law which structures the sphere of Is; and peripheral imputation is the normative analogue of causality. It is a purely theoretical category and has no addressee.

A second kind of theoretical Ought can be found in the concept of validity: The validity of any logical judgment is given if one 'ought' to think in accordance with it. The practical Ought, contained especially in the concept of 'duty,' which has an addressee, is shunted off to the disposable level of secondary norms.

The third phase, between around 1940 and 1960, is heralded by the abandonment of the idealistic neo-Kantian conception of cognition in favor of a more or less implicit commonsense realism. Now, Kelsen takes the legal norm to be "given" to legal cognition and "described" by the judgment of legal science, the *Rechtssatz*. He avoids labelling it as an ideal or abstract entity and tends toward legal realism. The sphere of Ought remains vague, and the explanation of the dualism of Is and Ought dwindles to the thesis that it is impossible that something which ought to be follows from something that is, and vice versa. "Ought" is a portmanteau concept, covering very different normative functions such as commanding, prohibiting, empowering, etc. Peripheral imputation steps back as normative operator of the general legal norm, and empowerment takes its place. All "practical" manifestations of the Ought in law, that is, normative demands for a certain action, are once more a matter of reducible secondary norms. Norms are taken to be the meaning-contents of intentional acts; as they are not assertions, there is no direct logic of norms. However, Kelsen introduces the dubious notion of an "indirect" logic of norms – a theory of logical relations between norms which are somehow a projection from the relations between judgments or statements describing norms.

The writings of the fourth phase, lasting until Kelsen's death in 1973, can be seen as an attempt to resolve the inconsistencies of the third phase. They are characterized by a strict will theory of norms. For the first time in his career, Kelsen maintains that any Ought or norm is impossible without an act of will as its bearer. The will even seems to be part of the definition of the Ought. But this is at odds with Kelsen's assumption that the Ought is objective. Furthermore, partly because of his will theory of norms and partly because of his sticking to the thesis that norms are objects "given" to cognition, Kelsen abandons the notion that there may be any direct or indirect logical relations between norms. Normativism, which flourished abundantly in Kelsen's neo-Kantian period, is practically gone.

Finally, a very short appraisal. I hope to have shown that the general philosophical normativistic approach can be well argued for. As Kant demonstrated, in respect of the aim of preserving objectivity of cognition, it is the least demanding alternative to an untenable position of philosophical realism according to which cognition deals with a "world-in-itself." Furthermore, normativism is able to thwart any naturalistic attempt to reduce cognition to physiological or psychical processes. Lotze's terse argument for this case given in Section 2.3.1 seems to be unanswerable; and it is still applicable in what seems to be a reincarnation of the debate about psychologism – the current debate about the role of cognitive sciences.

Kelsen's version of legal-theoretical normativism, however, is too complex to admit of a simple assessment. His theory began as a methodology of legal dogmatics, as embodied in legal practice, and developed into a rational reconstruction of the *factum* of legal science in his neo-Kantian phase. In this program, normativism defines not only the institutionalized perspective of lawyers, but also the view one has to take if law as a distinct object of cognition is to be possible at all. This is largely plausible, and maybe the Pure Theory in its neo-Kantian guise offers the best background for any attempt to reconcile the normativity, the objectivity, and the positivity of the law. Yet, Kelsen's normativism is obscured by his tendency to merge different aspects which should be kept apart. He does not clearly distinguish between (1) the prescientific 'practical' normativity which is contained in 'everyday' legal discourse about rights, duties, etc.; (2) the 'theoretical' Ought (be it the construed will of the state, imputation, or empowerment) which is contained in the primary legal norm as a product of cognitive activity and distinguishes law from other phenomena; and (3) the even less substantial Ought making up the validity of any cognitive judgment. And he does not succeed in determining the relation between Ought and willing in an unequivocal way.

But perhaps it is exactly such ambiguities and inconsistencies which, together with its critical attitude, make up the never-ending topicality and fertility of the Pure Theory.

References

Beiser, F. C. (2009). Normativity in Neo-Kantianism: Its Rise and Fall. *International Journal of Philosophical Studies* (17), 9–27.

Beiser, F. C. (2013). *Late German Idealism: Trendelenburg & Lotze*. Oxford: Oxford University Press.

Beiser, F. C. (2014). *The Genesis of Neo-Kantianism, 1796–1880*. Oxford: Oxford University Press.

Bennett, K. and McLaughlin, B. (2018). Supervenience. In *Stanford Encyclopedia of Philosophy*, https://plato.stanford.edu/entries/superveni ence/ (accessed October 14, 2020).

Frege, G. (1986). Der Gedanke. In Gottlob Frege, *Logische Untersuchungen*, ed. by G. Patzig, 3rd ed. Göttingen: Vandenhoeck & Ruprecht, 30–53.

Habermas, J. (1999). *Wahrheit und Rechtfertigung*. Frankfurt/Main: Suhrkamp.

Hart, H. L. A. (1961). *The Concept of Law*. Oxford: Clarendon Press.

Heidemann, C. (1997). *Die Norm als Tatsache. Zur Normentheorie Hans Kelsens*. Baden-Baden: Nomos Verlag.

Heidemann, C. (1999). Norms, Facts, and Judgments. A Reply to S. L. Paulson. *Oxford Journal of Legal Studies* (19), 345–50.

Heidemann, C. (2000). The Creation of Normative Facts. *Law and Philosophy* (19), 263–81.

Heidemann, C. (2007). Noch einmal: Stanley L. Paulson und Kelsens urteilstheoretischer Normbegriff. *Archiv für Rechts- und Sozialphilosophie* (93), 345–62.

Heidemann, C. (2020). Das Faktum der Rechtswissenschaft bei Hans Kelsen. In M. Jestaedt, R. Poscher, and J. Kammerhofer, eds., *Die Reine Rechtslehre auf dem Prüfstand. Hans Kelsen's Pure Theory of Law: Conceptions and Misconceptions*. Stuttgart: Franz Steiner Verlag, 81–98.

Hoeschen, A. (1999). *Das "Dostojewsky"-Projekt. Lukács neukantianisches Frühwerk in seinem ideengeschichtlichen Kontext*. Tübingen: de Gruyter.

Hume, D. (2007a). *A Treatise of Human Nature*. Oxford: Clarendon Press.

Hume, D. (2007b). *An Enquiry Concerning Human Understanding*. Oxford: Oxford University Press.

Husserl, E. (1900). *Logische Untersuchungen*, Vol. 1. Leipzig: Veit & Comp.

Kant, I. (1992). The Jäsche logic. In I. Kant, *Lectures on Logic*, trans. and ed. by J. M. Young. Cambridge: Cambridge University Press, 521–640.

Kant, I. (1998). *Critique of Pure Reason*, trans. and ed. by P. Guyer and A. W. Wood. Cambridge: Cambridge University Press.

Kant, I. (2002). *Critique of the Power of Judgment*, trans. and ed. by P. Guyer and E. Matthews. Cambridge: Cambridge University Press.

Kant, I. (2004). *Prolegomena to Any Future Metaphysics*, trans. and ed. by G. Hatfield. Cambridge: Cambridge University Press.

Kant, I. (2015). *Critique of Practical Reason*, trans. and ed. by M. Gregor, revised ed. Cambridge: Cambridge University Press.

Kelsen, H. (1911). *Hauptprobleme der Staatsrechtslehre*. Tübingen: Mohr.

Kelsen, H. (1920). *Das Problem der Souveränität und die Theorie des Völkerrechts*. Tübingen: Mohr.

Kelsen, H. (1922a). Rechtswissenschaft und Recht. Erledigung eines Versuchs zur Überwindung der "Rechtsdogmatik." *ZöR* (3), 103–235.

Kelsen, H. (1922b). *Der soziologische und der juristische Staatsbegriff*. Tübingen: Mohr.

Kelsen, H. (1923). *Hauptprobleme der Staatsrechtslehre*, 2nd ed. Tübingen: Mohr.

Kelsen, H. (1925). *Allgemeine Staatslehre*. Berlin: Springer.

Kelsen, H. (1928a). *Die philosophischen Grundlagen der Naturrechtslehre und des Rechtspositivismus*. Berlin: Pan-Verlag.

Kelsen, H. (1928b). *Rechtsgeschichte gegen Rechtsphilosophie? Eine Erwiderung*. Vienna: Julius Springer.

Kelsen, H. (1934). *Reine Rechtslehre. Einleitung in die rechtswissenschaftliche Problematik*. Leipzig and Vienna: Deuticke.

Kelsen, H. (1939). Die Entstehung des Kausalgesetzes aus dem Vergeltungsprinzip. *The Journal of Unified Science (Erkenntnis)* 8, 69–130.

Kelsen, H. (1941). *Vergeltung und Kausalität*. The Hague: W. P. van Stockum.

Kelsen, H. (1957a). The Pure Theory of Law and Analytical Jurisprudence. In H. Kelsen, *What Is Justice? Justice, Law and Politics in the Mirror of Science. Collected Essays by Hans Kelsen*. Berkeley and Los Angeles: University of California Press, 266–87.

Kelsen, H. (1957b). Why Should the Law Be Obeyed? In H. Kelsen, *What Is Justice? Justice, Law and Politics in the Mirror of Science. Collected Essays by Hans Kelsen*. Berkeley and Los Angeles: University of California Press, 257–65.

Kelsen, H. (1960). *Reine Rechtslehre*, 2nd ed. Vienna: Deuticke.

Kelsen, H. (1963). Die Grundlagen der Naturrechtslehre. *ÖZöR* (13), 1–37.

Kelsen, H. (1968a). Das Verhältnis von Staat und Recht im Lichte der Erkenntniskritik. In H. Klecatsky, R. Marcic, and H. Schambeck, eds., *Die Wiener Rechtstheoretische Schule*. Vienna: Europa-Verlag, 77–120.

Kelsen, H. (1968b). Die Rechtswissenschaft als Normwissenschaft oder als Kulturwissenschaft. In H. Klecatsky, R. Marcic, and H. Schambeck, eds., *Die Wiener Rechtstheoretische Schule*. Vienna: Europa-Verlag, 31–77.

Kelsen, H. (1968c). Die Problematik der Reinen Rechtslehre. *ÖZöR* (18), 143–84.

Kelsen, H. (1968d). Die Funktion der Verfassung. In H. Klecatsky, R. Marcic, and H. Schambeck, eds., *Die Wiener Rechtstheoretische Schule*. Vienna: Europa-Verlag, 1615–22.

Kelsen, H. (1979). *Allgemeine Theorie der Normen*, ed. by K. Ringhofer and R. Walter. Viena: Manz.

Kelsen, H. (1991). *General Theory of Norms*, trans. by M. Hartney. Oxford: Clarendon Press.

Kelsen, H. (1992). *Introduction to the Problems of Legal Theory*, trans. and ed. by B. Litschewski Paulson and S. L. Paulson. Oxford: Clarendon Press.

Kelsen, H. (1998a). Foreword to Hauptprobleme der Staatsrechtslehre, trans. by S. L. Paulson. In S. L. Paulson and B. Litschewski Paulson, eds., *Normativity and Norms*. Oxford: Clarendon Press, 3–22.

Kelsen, H. (1998b) A Letter to Renato Treves, trans. by S. L. Paulson. In S. L. Paulson and B. Litschewski Paulson, eds., *Normativity and Norms*. Oxford: Clarendon Press, 169–76.

Kelsen, H. (2005). *The Pure Theory of Law*, trans. from the 2nd ed. by M. Knight. Clark, NJ: The Lawbook Exchange.

Kelsen, H. (2006). Autobiographie (1947). In M. Jestaedt, ed., *Hans Kelsen im Selbstzeugnis*. Tübingen: Mohr Siebeck.

Kelsen, H. and Klug, U. (1981). *Rechtsnormen und logische Analyse. Ein Briefwechsel 1959 bis 1965*. Vienna: Deuticke.

Köhnke, K. C. (1993). *Entstehung und Aufstieg des Neukantianismus*. Frankfurt: Suhrkamp.

Kubeš, V. (1980). Das neueste Werk Hans Kelsens über die allgemeine Theorie der Normen und die Zukunft der Reinen Rechtslehre. *ÖZöR* (31), 155–99.

Lotze, H. (1841). *Metaphysik*. Leipzig: Weidmann'sche Buchhandlung.

Lotze, H. (1884). *Logics*, trans. and ed. by B. Bosanquet. Oxford: Clarendon Press.

McIntyre, A. C. (1959). Hume on "Is" and "Ought." *The Philosophical Review* (68), 451–68.

Merkl, A. J. (1917). Das Recht im Lichte seiner Auslegung. *Deutsche Richterzeitung* (9), 162–76.

Nino, C. S. (1998). Some Confusions Surrounding Kelsen's Concept of Validity. In S. L. Paulson and B. Litschewski Paulson, eds., *Normativity and Norms*. Oxford: Clarendon Press, 253–62.

Opałek, K. (1980). *Überlegungen zu Hans Kelsens "Allgemeiner Theorie der Normen."* Vienna: Manz.

Paulson, S. L. (1988a). Die Rezeption Kelsens in Amerika. In O. Weinberger and W. Krawietz, eds., *Die Reine Rechtslehre im Spiegel ihrer Fortsetzer und Kritiker*. Vienna and New York: Springer, 179–202.

Paulson, S. L. (1988b). An Empowerment Theory of Legal Norms. *Ratio Juris* (1), 58–72.

Paulson, S. L. (1990). Towards a Periodization of the Pure Theory of Law. In L. Gianformaggio, ed., *Hans Kelsen's Legal Theory. A Diachronic Point of View*. Turin: Giappichelli editore.

Paulson, S. L. (2000). On the Puzzle Surrounding Hans Kelsen's Basic Norm. *Ratio Juris* (13), 279–93.

Paulson, S. L. (2012). A "Justified Normativity" Thesis in Hans Kelsen's Pure Theory of Law? In M. Klatt. ed., *Institutionalized Reason. The Jurisprudence of Robert Alexy*. Oxford: Oxford University Press, 61–114.

Paulson, S. L. (2013). Hans Kelsen: Das Ende der Reinen Rechtslehre? Ein Briefwechsel, ein Spannungsverhältnis und der Umsturz der Rechtslehre Hans Kelsens. In St. Augsberg and A. Funke, eds., *Kölner Juristen im 20. Jahrhundert*. Tübingen: Mohr Siebeck, 53–74.

Paulson, S. L. (2017). Hans Kelsen and Carl Schmitt: Growing Discord, Culminating in the "Guardian" Controversy of 1931. In J. Meierhenrich and O. Simons, eds., *The Oxford Handbook of Carl Schmitt*. Oxford: Oxford University Press, 510–46.

Raz, J. (1974). Kelsen's Theory of the Basic Norm. *American Journal of Jurisprudence* (19), 94–111.

Rickert, H. (1909). Zwei Wege der Erkenntnistheorie. *Kant-Studien* (14), 169–228.

Rickert, H. (1921). *Der Gegenstand der Erkenntnis*, 4th and 5th ed. Tübingen: Mohr.

Ross, A. (1957). Review of Hans Kelsen, "What Is Justice?". *California Law Review* (45), 564–70.

Schmitt, C. (1977). Über die drei Arten des rechtswissenschaftlichen Denkens. In H.-J. Koch, ed., *Die juristische Methode im Staatsrecht*. Frankfurt/Main: Suhrkamp, 366–98.

Thieme, K. (1887). *Der Primat der praktischen Vernunft*. Leipzig: Ackermann & Glaser. https://archive.org/details/derprimatderprak00thie/mode/2up (accessed August 20, 2021).

Walker, R. C. S. (2017). The Primacy of Practical Reason. In M. C. Altman, ed., *The Palgrave Kant Handbook*. London: Springer Nature, 191–209.

Weinberger, O. (1981). *Normentheorie als Grundlage der Jurisprudenz und Ethik*. Berlin: Duncker & Humblot.

Willaschek, M. (2009). Rationale Postulate. Über Kants These vom Primat der praktischen reinen Vernunft. In H. F. Klemme, ed., *Kant und die Zukunft der europäischen Aufklärung*. Berlin and New York: de Gruyter, 251–68.

Willaschek, M. (2010). Die "Spontaneität des Erkenntnisses." Über die Abhängigkeit der "Transzendentalen Analytik" von der Auflösung der Dritten Antinomie. In J. Chotaš, J. Karásek, and J. Stolzenberg, eds., *Metaphysik und Kritik. Interpretationen zur "Transzendentalen Dialektik."* Würzburg: Königshausen und Neumann, 165–84.

Windelband, W. (1874). Review of Christoph Sigwart, Logik. *Philosophische Monatshefte* (10), 33–42.

Windelband, W. (1907). *Präludien*, 3rd ed. Tübingen: Mohr.

Windelband, W. (1912). *Prinzipien der Logik*. Tübingen: Mohr.

Wittgenstein, L. (2009). *Philosophical Investigations*. German text with an English trans. by G. E. M. Anscombe, P. M. S. Hacker, and J. Schulte, revised 4th ed. by P. M. S. Hacker and J. Schulte. Chichester, UK: Wiley-Blackwell.

Zalewska, M. (2020a). The Basic Norm at the Time of the Revolution. In M. Belov and A. A. i Ninet, eds., *Revolution, Transition, Memory, and Oblivion*. Cheltenham, UK: Edward Elgar Publishing.

Zalewska, M. (2020b). Does Hans Kelsen's Pure Theory of Law Support Rule of Law and Democracy? In H. Takikawa, ed., *The Rule of Law and Democracy. The 12th Kobe Lecture and the 1st IVR Japan International Conference*. Stuttgart: Franz Steiner, 203–16.

Cambridge Elements ≡

Elements in the Philosophy of Law

Series Editors

George Pavlakos
University of Glasgow

George Pavlakos is Professor of Law and Philosophy at the School of Law, University of Glasgow. He has held visiting posts at the universities of Kiel and Luzern, the European University Institute, the UCLA Law School, the Cornell Law School and the Beihang Law School in Beijing. He is the author of *Our Knowledge of the Law* (2007) and more recently has co-edited *Agency, Negligence and Responsibility* (2021) and *Reasons and Intentions in Law and Practical Agency* (2015).

Gerald J. Postema
University of North Carolina at Chapel Hill

Gerald J. Postema is Professor Emeritus of Philosophy at the University of North Carolina at Chapel Hill. Among his publications count *Utility, Publicity, and Law: Bentham's Moral and Legal Philosophy* (2019); *On the Law of Nature, Reason, and the Common Law: Selected Jurisprudential Writings of Sir Matthew Hale* (2017); *Legal Philosophy in the Twentieth Century: The Common Law World* (2011), *Bentham and the Common Law Tradition, 2nd edition* (2019).

Kenneth M. Ehrenberg
University of Surrey

Kenneth M. Ehrenberg is Reader in Public Law and Legal Theory at the University of Surrey School of Law and Co-Director of the Surrey Centre for Law and Philosophy. He is the author of *The Functions of Law* (2016) and numerous articles on the nature of law, jurisprudential methodology, the relation of law to morality, practical authority, and the epistemology of evidence law.

Associate Editor

Sally Zhu
University of Sheffield

Sally Zhu is a Lecturer in Property Law at University of Sheffield. Her research is on property and private law aspects of platform and digital economies.

About the Series

This series provides an accessible overview of the philosophy of law, drawing on its varied intellectual traditions in order to showcase the interdisciplinary dimensions of jurisprudential enquiry, review the state of the art in the field, and suggest fresh research agendas for the future.

Focussing on issues rather than traditions or authors, each contribution seeks to deepen our understanding of the foundations of the law, ultimately with a view to offering practical insights into some of the major challenges of our age.

Cambridge Elements $\equiv$

Elements in the Philosophy of Law

Elements in the Series

Hans Kelsen's Normativism
Carsten Heidemann

A full series listing is available at: www.cambridge.org/EPHL

Printed in the United States
by Baker & Taylor Publisher Services